PREACHING JUSTICE

PREACHING JUSTICE

ETHNIC AND

CULTURAL

PERSPECTIVES

EDITED BY
CHRISTINE MARIE SMITH

UNITED CHURCH PRESS
Cleveland, Ohio

With gratitude for

Spirit of the Lakes United Church of Christ,

Minneapolis, Minnesota

United Church Press, Cleveland, Ohio 44115
© 1998 by Christine Marie Smith

Story of Sig used by permission of Rev. Meredyth Bellows. • "Breaking Silence" by Janice Mirikitani. Reprinted from *Shedding Silence* by Janice Mirikitani. © Copyright 1987 by Janice Mirikitani. • From Martin Niemoeller, in *The Six Days of Destruction: Meditations toward Hope,* ed. Elie Wiesel and Albert H. Friedlander (New York: Paulist Press, 1988). Reprinted by permission of Paulist Press. • "Playing Cards with the Jailer" by Mitsuye Yamada. Reprinted by permission of the author.

Biblical quotations, except where otherwise noted, are from the New Revised Standard Version of the Bible, © 1989 by the Division of Christian Education of the National Council of the Churches of Christ in the U.S.A., and are used by permission

03 02 01 00 99 98   5 4 3 2 1

LIBRARY OF CONGRESS CATALOGING-IN-PUBLICATION DATA

Preaching justice : ethnic and cultural perspectives / edited by Christine M. Smith.
    p. cm.
    Includes bibliographical references.
    ISBN 0-8298-1291-1 (pbk. : alk. paper)
    1. Preaching.   2. Religion and justice.   3. Minorities — Religious life.
I. Smith, Christine M. (Christine Marie), 1953– .
BV4221.P74   1998
251'.008 — dc21

98-26012
CIP

Contents

Acknowledgments

I WANT TO THANK EACH ONE of the authors individually, and all of them together. I am enormously grateful for each of their contributions and for their willingness to participate in this distinctive homiletical venture. Each of their voices is unique, and each of their perspectives on preaching justice will urge us to deepen our understandings of the preaching task and expand our vision and hope of a transformed world. For each one of their voices, and for all the voices and lives yet to make their impact on how and why we preach, I give thanks.

I want to especially thank Timothy G. Staveteig, editor of The Pilgrim Press. He has a rare vision of faith and justice that permeates all his work. This faithful vision enabled him to immediately understand and support a homiletical project that would focus upon voices and communities that continue to be marginalized and silenced by the larger church. His vision not only supported and encouraged this project, but also participated in its birth.

The community of United Theological Seminary has been generous in its support of my scholarly commitments and my larger work in the world. I am profoundly grateful for this liberating context in which I can teach, and from which I can write, speak, and preach as an "out" lesbian of the Christian church.

I share my daily life with Cathie Crooks, a theologian, minister, and wonderful preacher in her own right. I am grateful for her critical editing of my chapter, the passionate sense of Christian vocation we share together, and, most especially, her sustaining love.

Contributors

Kathy Black is associate professor of homiletics and liturgics at Claremont School of Theology in southern California. She is a United Methodist minister and a sign language interpreter, and she has pastored a Deaf congregation. Her publications include *A Healing Homiletic: Preaching and Disabilities* and *Worship Across Cultures* (forthcoming, Abingdon Press, 1998).

Martin Brokenleg is a professor of Native American studies at Augustana College in Sioux Falls, South Dakota. He is an enrolled member of the Rosebud Sioux tribe, an Episcopal priest, and a therapist. A published author on young people at risk, he works with men's groups and gay/lesbian people. He lives with his partner, Gene Sederstrom.

Teresa Fry Brown is assistant professor of homiletics and interim director of the Black Church Studies Program at Candler School of Theology, Emory University, Atlanta, Georgia. She is an ordained minister in the African Methodist Episcopal Church, and has published sermons and articles in *Those Preachin' Women* and *The Abingdon Women's Preaching Annual*.

Eleazar S. Fernandez is associate professor of constructive theology at United Theological Seminary of the Twin Cities. He received his theological studies from Union Theological Seminary in the Philippines (M.Div.), Princeton Theological Seminary (Th.M.), and Vanderbilt University (Ph.D.). Before coming to the United States he served in the pastorate under the United Church of Christ in the Philippines and in various ecumenical bodies in that country. He now has dual ministerial standing with UCC-Philippines and UCC-USA. His most recent publication is *Toward a Theology of Struggle*.

Justo L. González is a United Methodist minister and a member of the Rio Grande Conference. He is a church historian, whose best-known books in that field are *A History of Christian Thought* (three volumes) and *The Story of Christianity* (two volumes). Jointly with his spouse, Catherine Gunsalus González (professor of church history at Columbia Theological Seminary), he has published *The Liberating Pulpit* as well as several other pieces on homiletics. He is currently executive director of the Hispanic Initiative at Emory University, Atlanta, Georgia.

Eunjoo Mary Kim is an adjunct professor of preaching at New Brunswick Theological Seminary. She has been called by the New Garden Korean Presbyterian Church (U.S.A.) in Ridgewood, New Jersey, and has served as the pastor for the English-speaking congregation. She received her master's degree in New Testament theology at Ewha Women's University in Korea and M.Div. and Ph.D. degrees at Princeton Theological Seminary. She is the first and so far only Asian to earn a Ph.D. degree in the field of homiletics.

Stacy Offner is the rabbi of Shir Tikvah Congregation, a synagogue serving the Twin Cities of St. Paul and Minneapolis. Her sermons have been published in *Sacred Strands* and *Sermons by Minnesota Women*. She serves as adjunct professor of Jewish ethics at Hamline University, and lives in St. Paul with her partner, Nancy Abramson.

Christine Marie Smith is a professor of preaching and worship at United Theological Seminary of the Twin Cities, Minneapolis, Minnesota. She served as the president of the Academy of Homiletics during 1997. She is a United Church of Christ clergyperson and the author of *Weaving the Sermon: Preaching from a Feminist Perspective* and *Preaching as Weeping, Confession, and Resistance: Radical Responses to Radical Evil.*

The Craft and
Act of Preaching Justice

FROM BEGINNING TO END this book has been a collective piece of work. This volume was envisioned as a scholarly contribution that would focus on the distinctive voices emerging from within communities of ethnicity and culture, and the implications of those voices for the act of preaching justice. Each of the authors clearly "caught" that vision and graciously agreed to join the project.

A volume of this kind does not currently exist in the field of homiletics. This volume brings together eight very diverse voices from eight different cultural/ethnic communities and asks them to take up the opportunity and challenge of giving expression to some of the particular justice concerns, issues, and passions that give rise to a preaching ministry within one's community and beyond any one particular community. This volume puts before us voices that promise to change the field of homiletics, and the craft and practice of preaching.

As a homiletician and a teacher of preachers, I am constantly aware that Euro-American voices still dominate every aspect of the field of homiletics. This is not just a scholarly, theoretical issue for me; this is an issue of justice. As diverse as the voices from within Euro-American culture may be, when one cultural perspective completely dominates an entire pastoral and theological field, radical change is needed. I envision this volume actively participating in that essential change.

After the authors were secured, each one of them received six guiding questions. The questions reveal the specific agenda of the volume:

1. What is your understanding of preaching as an act of ministry?
2. Describe your social location. What might be distinct or significant about your particular voice and perspective?

3. What has been your actual experience of observing, studying, or practicing the art and craft of preaching within your community?
4. What are some of the social and cultural injustices within your particular community that compel you to "preach justice"?
5. What are some of the primary deconstructive and constructive theological tasks facing preachers within your community?
6. Name and describe distinct images/metaphors for "preaching justice"
that arise from within the struggle and human agency of your community.

Because each woman or man who preaches has a very particular understanding of preaching as an act of ministry, the first question seemed to be
the logical and obvious place for the authors to begin. Some of the authors
articulate their understanding of the act of preaching in the context of a
very particular cultural story, metaphor, or image; some within a historical-
cultural context; still others within a broader understanding of pastoral
ministry. Some of the authors' understandings of preaching as an act of
ministry are utterly contextualized within those authors' cultural/ethnic
communities; others express an understanding of preaching that has implications for their cultural/ethnic community while remaining at the same
time less contextualized. The question is a very broad and open one, and
the authors have articulated in rich and diverse ways their understanding
of preaching as an act of ministry.

Next, each author was asked to describe her or his social location, and to
name some elements of her or his particular preaching voice that might
bring distinctive or significant dimensions to the act of preaching. Each
author identified key components of her or his social, ethnic, cultural, and
ecclesiastical identities that shape and inform preaching. Though it is not
always so, all preachers should be able to not only describe their social
location, but also articulate significant ways in which their social location
influences their biblical hermeneutics, their theological thinking, their
pastoral sensitivities, and their homiletical methodologies. Such a correction lies at the heart of this volume.

From my years of teaching preaching, and from my work with religious
leaders and preachers in the United States and in Canada, I make the following observation about preachers and social location: preachers who are
from within cultural and ethnic communities that are marginalized, and/
or communities that experience forms of social and ecclesiastical oppression, usually are better able to articulate the impact of social location on

every dimension of their preaching. Preachers who are Americans or Canadians of European descent, and who experience many of the privileges of ethnicity and class, find it much more difficult to name dimensions of their social location and the ramifications of those dimensions on their preaching ministry.

It is not happenstance that preachers who experience the privileges of ethnicity, class, heterosexual, and able-bodied realities find it more difficult to describe their social location. People who are marginalized, oppressed, or disenfranchised constantly experience the oppressive impact of social location in their daily lives, and they must be aware of its impact in order to survive. In contrast, for the more privileged, social location is often a reality that can simply be lived and not thought about or reflected upon. For people of European descent, and for heterosexual and able-bodied people, naming and articulating how one's social location affects one's life, ministry, and preaching is an act of justice. In this act, one decentralizes one's identity from the assumed norm, and attempts to take responsibility for the limited, prejudicial, and often oppressive dimensions of one's human identity in relation to the rest of humanity. For persons who are African American, Korean American, Filipino American, disabled, lesbian/gay, Native American, Jewish, or Hispanic/Latino/Latina, the act of describing social location is more an act of empowerment, an act of naming the distinctive gifts, understandings, worldviews, and communities that give rise to one's particular life, ministry, and preaching. Because all of the authors-preachers within this volume come from communities that are significantly marginalized in our culture, their social location descriptions need to receive more attention and be given more authority in the shaping and reshaping of the ministry of preaching. The hope is that all who read this volume will be reminded of the primacy of social location in preaching and will be challenged to become ever more astute at identifying and claiming those critical dimensions of human identity.

The third question continues to build upon the issue of social location, focusing specifically on how the authors' communities have been primary agents of influence on the evolution of their skills and self-understanding as preachers. Women and men reading these descriptions will be inspired to reflect upon the communities that have fundamentally shaped their own preaching voices and how they remain accountable to those particular communities throughout their ministries. This accountability may take the form of affirmation and connection, or it may involve critique and resistance.

The fourth question asks the authors-preachers to clearly and boldly name some of the many forms of oppression their communities experience. In the naming of social and cultural injustices, the authors share the social analysis that undergirds their preaching ministries: that is, how they understand the social, economic, ecclesiastical, and political realities that have a direct impact on their communities. These are some of the realities, some of the human faces of injustice, that compel each one of us to "preach justice." In the midst of so many churches struggling to find meaning, purpose, and a strong sense of mission, and in the face of what feels like rampant religious lethargy and bigotry in this country, some of us as preachers may feel appropriately indicted by the passion and urgency behind the authors' descriptions of those injustices that compel us to preach.

The authors were then asked to address the primary deconstructive and constructive theological tasks facing preachers within their particular communities. For marginalized and oppressed individuals and communities, this task is complex. The "deconstructive" task asks preachers to honestly critique their traditions, naming ways Christianity and Judaism have participated in the oppression of some of their own people, and to honestly state what must be resisted and changed about the traditions to make them more just. The "constructive" task asks preachers to name and construct the kind of new theological thinking that might participate in the transformation of the religious tradition within which they stand as well as the larger structures and institutions of our society. This naming and constructing is in itself an act of justice. Marginalized and oppressed people name and construct reality from the locus of their lives, yet these acts often are done in the confines of their particular community. The larger, more public power of naming and constructing reality, in ways that influence and shape our collective social and ecclesiastical lives, is the power that has been stolen and denied. This volume in general, and this question in particular, seeks to enable these individual preachers, and the communities out of which they arise, to claim this public power of critiquing, naming, and constructing social and religious meaning. This section certainly invites, and might even compel, other preachers to engage in such serious deconstructive and constructive theological and homiletical work.

Finally, the authors-preachers were asked to describe any distinct images and/or metaphors for "preaching justice" that arise from within the struggle and human agency of their particular communities. The belief that people are greatly influenced and shaped by the images and metaphors they hold about reality indicated the need to experience the images and metaphors that inform and instill identity and hope in the lives of these eight preachers. The images shared by each author are distinct, yet all of them invite us into an eschatological hope for a transformed and just world. These images convey what the authors long for, hope for, believe in, and preach regarding justice. No matter what our particular worldview and cultural community, many of these final images will challenge our traditional biblical interpretations, our theological constructs, our ecclesiastical realities, and our social and cultural assumptions. These contexualized images of preaching urge all preachers to clarify and acknowledge the images and metaphors that fundamentally inform both the content and the style of their preaching ministries.

The authors-preachers have addressed these six guiding questions in both direct and indirect ways. There is no uniformity in the chapters, and each chapter reads in its own unique way. You will be frustrated if you seek to find the six guiding questions answered in a similar format chapter by chapter. You will be enlightened and changed if you allow each author to enter into the substance of the questions in her or his particular way, and thus to demonstrate the assumption upon which the volume is constructed: each preaching voice is distinct, and each ethnic and cultural community from which a preacher emerges is profoundly particular. This is the truth you will discover within these pages, and this truth means that you will find homiletical insights you had not imagined and a diversity of preaching perspectives that will humble and challenge you. May these voices, and the indictments and visions they represent, compel us all to preach justice.

CHAPTER ONE

A Perspective of the Disabled

TRANSFORMING IMAGES OF GOD, INTERDEPENDENCE, AND HEALING

KATHY BLACK

THE ACT OF PREACHING is both a privilege and a responsibility. What we proclaim from the pulpit has the potential for shaping beliefs and enacting change. Whether members of the congregation or synagogue understand themselves to be persons of power or persons on the margins of society, what we preach has the power to mobilize people to encounter the face of God in persons from ethnicities and cultures different from our own. This recognition provides a foundation for seeking justice in our diverse world.

You may be wondering what a chapter about preaching justice among persons with disabilities is doing in a book about ethnicity and culture. It is a complicated issue, but it certainly is an issue of justice. How we preach the biblical narratives that deal with persons who are blind or deaf or have leprosy can be healing or oppressive for persons with those disabilities today. Most persons with disabilities are not found in separate congregations. They are found in almost every congregation, crossing all ethnic and cultural boundaries.

DISABLED AS A DISTINCT CULTURE?

Persons who experience severe vision loss, paralysis, mental illness, hearing loss, chronic illness, and numerous other debilitating diseases such as cancer and AIDS are all considered persons with disabilities. Yet only deaf persons born to deaf parents are considered members of a particular culture—the Deaf culture, which has its own language, value system, and visual way of perceiving the world. Most of society believes that anyone who is deaf is living with a *disability*, but those who grew up in a deaf family and learned sign language from birth are really part of a cultural, linguistic minority (like other ethnic groups in this country) and do not see themselves as persons with disabilities.

The common experience of deafness also tends to override ethnicity and race, especially in regard to one's choice of a worshiping community. In the many Deaf churches throughout the country, persons from various ethnicities will be present. This is not to say that racism is not present in the Deaf community but that the need for sign language and a visual style of worship draws persons from various ethnic cultures to Deaf churches. Sociologists, anthropologists, and linguists have all documented the existence of this Deaf culture.[1] Therefore, one can make a strong argument for including the Deaf culture in a book about ethnicity and culture. The case for including all persons with disabilities in a book about preaching justice in various ethnic and cultural contexts is much more complex, yet in many ways, more needed because of a lack of collective identity.

Let me say a word about my choice of the term "persons with disabilities." In attempts to name in positive ways the life experiences of persons with disabilities, a few other terms have gone in and out of vogue in the past fifteen years or more: "handicapped," "handicapping conditions," "differently abled," and "physically challenged." I have struggled with these terms for years now to identify those I have been in ministry with and to identify myself. I honor people's right to choose the term that is most comfortable for themselves and their situation. Politically, I use the term "persons with disabilities" because the United Nations Decade for Persons with Disabilities (1980–90) used that term, and now the Americans with Disabilities Act has followed suit. It has become one term that has the capability of unifying the diverse community rather than dividing it under various terms.

SOCIAL LOCATION AND PERSONAL IDENTITY

For myself, I have finally decided that I am, first, a person and, second, someone with a disability. I am a Euro-American, middle-class, United Methodist clergywoman, but I am also a person with a disability. Raised on a toxic-waste dump, I have a disability that most probably stems from toxic damage to my central and autonomic nervous systems. At its worst, I experience episodes of total but temporary flaccid paralysis. I cannot move, open my eyes, or speak. I am conscious, however—I can hear and feel. More often I experience times of severe weakness of the muscles, which makes walking and standing difficult. At various times I use a walker with a seat or an electric three-wheel cart.

My disability happens to be physical; therefore, I often feel physically challenged, but that term tends to omit those whose disability is from some form of mental or psychological illness rather than physical. I have also come to believe that good intentions of the able-bodied folk who use alternative terms may deny a major aspect of who we are by trying to pretend in some way that the disability does not matter. For some, that may be true. But for most people I know who live with a disability, it is an integral part of who they are and, on a daily basis, cannot be denied. I am a person first, but I do have a disability. It is often hidden from public view, but it is never absent from my mind, and the choices I make are based on how my actions may affect—in my case, trigger—the disability.

I will also precede any description of a disability with the word "person." Although I experience episodes of paralysis and severe weakness of the muscles, I am also a seminary professor and a strong feminist. I spent seven years pastoring in the Deaf community, preaching in sign language every week. Many aspects of my life contribute to my current identity as a person. My disability is only one facet.

Therefore, I will use phrases such as "person who is blind" and "person who is hard of hearing," except in the case of those who are culturally Deaf where "Deaf" is understood as a cultural, linguistic minority group. Persons who are culturally Deaf are proud of their deafness and heritage. To say "I am Deaf" is a statement of identification and solidarity with all those who share the same linguistic and cultural history, mores, and values as well as the same struggles in society. It is the same as someone taking pride in her or his ethnic heritage: "I am Vietnamese" or "I am African American." One never hears "I am a *person* who is Korean" or "I am a *person* who is Tongan." To say "I am Hmong" is a statement of pride in one's heritage. It is different within the disability community, however. Too often terms such as "cripple" and "retarded" limit a person's identity to the disability.[2]

In Whose Image?

Historically, persons with disabilities did not have the same rights as able-bodied individuals and were often perceived as less than human. It was difficult for people to encounter the face of God in persons who were perceived to be less than whole. Theologically, it was hard to believe that persons with disabilities were made in the image of God. Like John Merrick, the "Elephant Man," many persons with severe disfigurements were paraded in circuses as stars of the "freak shows."[3] Surely, their claim of being fully human was suspect as they were put on display to scare *real* people. Laws were enacted that forbade persons with various disabilities from marrying or from inheriting property.

Persons with physical, psychological, and mental limitations are still suspect today. Ethical questions abound: Should persons with mental limitations be allowed to marry? If they marry, should they be allowed to have children? Are persons who are paralyzed from the neck down capable of raising children? Is physician-assisted suicide a feasible option to a life lived in a wheelchair where constant attendant care is necessary? Should fetuses with Down's syndrome be aborted? Should abortion be the method of choice for other disabilities identifiable in the womb? Will the person's life be productive enough to contribute to society, or will the person be a constant drain on family and social systems? Should a person without arms be allowed to be ordained? How will he or she baptize babies or distribute the communion elements? The basic humanity of persons with disabilities is questioned.

What makes us in the image of God? Who determines what constitutes being fully human and what does not? Is a person's disability the sum total of identity? Is human productivity the measuring rod by which a person's life is valued? Persons with disabilities have been perpetually treated as weak, dependent, and not fully whole. Thus, it is important that we as homileticians claim that persons with disabilities, like everyone else, are made in the image of God and are fully human. Therefore, "person" should precede any description of one's disability.

Preachers do not always recognize one's personhood before one's disability. Following the translators of the Bible, many sermons use terms such as "paralytic," "epileptic," "leper," "the blind and lame," as if the disability were the sole characteristic of each person's identity. Luke 17:1–19 is usually referred to as "the ten lepers." Mark 2:1–12 is known as "the paralytic." Nameless, who they are has been reduced to their disability. It is often not clear homiletically or theologically whether these biblical characters or persons with like disabilities today are understood as made in the image of God, holy people with the same gifts and graces God gives to all for the ministry of the church in the world.

DIVERSITY OF LIVED EXPERIENCE

While the social stigma of living with a disability is common across disabilities, the degree of the stigma and the needs and issues faced vary from disability to disability. Because my disability is mostly hidden from the public, the stigma I face is minimal compared to a person who lives with quadriplegia (paralysis from the neck down) or someone whose speech patterns are not understandable because she was born with cerebral palsy.

Although members of the Deaf culture congregate in separate churches where a visual worship style is conducted in sign language, and although there are a few worship services designed for persons who have cognitive limitations, for the most part, the tremendous diversity within the disability community is not conducive to segregated congregations. The needs and issues change with each disability. There is no language barrier that binds the persons together as in the Deaf community. The social stigma is a unifying experience, but one's way of being in the world is totally different depending on one's disability.

A clear example was the first gathering of what is now the United Methodist Association of Physically Challenged Ministers. What seemed to be a simple act of voting became extremely complicated. The minister who was running the business meeting was paralyzed from the waist down and used a wheelchair. Among the other members of the group were ministers, seminary students, and some laypersons with various disabilities. The presiding officer said, "All those in favor please . . ." What sign of assent would be possible among such diverse physical abilities? Raising one's hand was not possible because two or three present had no hands or arms. Saying aye placed a hardship on deaf participants who did not use their voice. Standing excluded not only the presiding officer, but also several other members of the group. Everyone's experience and way of being in the world were so different that communal activities were exciting but very frustrating and challenging.

It is true that persons who live with blindness (or any other disability) often have a particular perspective on the world and share many frustrations and needs in common with other persons whose disability is like their own. But persons who are blind need constant auditory or tactile stimulation and persons who are hard of hearing need visual stimulation. Persons who are paralyzed have architectural barriers that need to be removed for them to fully participate in the life of any congregation. There is no one language or culture, no one disability or common experience, that is sufficient enough for persons with varying disabilities to organize their own churches or even to have separate worship services designed for their needs.

LEVELS OF DISCRIMINATION

In any congregation there may be persons who are blind, hard of hearing, struggling with cancer or AIDS, or living with a chronic illness, a mental illness, or some form of paralysis. The social stigma that accompanies various disabilities is similar to the discrimination experienced by persons in different ethnic groups.

Among ethnic groups, discrimination is often based on the color of one's skin, one's culturally based behaviors, or one's ability/inability to pronounce English. Among persons with disabilities, discrimination is likewise based on one's physical appearance, although it is not necessarily the color of one's skin. It is the physical appearance of being in a wheelchair, or the facial features of someone with Down's syndrome, the spastic arms or legs from cerebral palsy, the use of a cane or guide dog, or the lack of hair or emaciated appearance from cancer.

Discrimination is also based on one's behavior, which in this case is not culturally based but disability based: talking to oneself as a result of some forms of mental illness, speaking too loudly when one is hard of hearing, needing to be fed by a caregiver, or, like me, holding on to trees, bushes, and walls while staggering across campus on legs that feel like jelly.

And like persons from other ethnic groups, persons with disabilities are discriminated against by reason of their ability/inability to pronounce English properly. Persons who are deaf are not mute, but they choose *not* to use their voice because it is often incomprehensible and people treat them as if they were mentally incapable as well. People with forms of paralysis that affect speech are likewise discriminated against.

Unfortunately, while persons with various disabilities often share common experiences of discrimination, the churches where they worship often do not take into consideration the issues they face and the justice they seek. If there were separate churches for persons with disabilities, pastored by someone with a disability, it would be a very different story. But these separate churches, even separate worship services, are rare indeed. The burden, then, is on every pastor in the country to understand the issues of preaching justice among persons with disabilities since every congregation in this country currently has or will someday have persons with disabilities among its worshipers.

PREACHING JUSTICE
WITHIN THE DEAF CULTURE AND COMMUNITY

Numerically, there are many more churches that use sign language interpreters to make "hearing worship" accessible to those with a variety of hearing loss than there are separate Deaf congregations that have a Deaf style of worship. The issues discussed in this section emerge out of Deaf churches but apply to any pastor who has deaf persons in her or his congregation.

Several Deaf churches throughout the country have a unique worship and preaching style. For many hearing people, it is difficult to imagine worship without speech and hearing. The organ prelude, the collective voice of the congregation in prayer, the oratory of the preacher, the choir lifting voices in harmony, and the congregation's hymns swelling in unison are all absent from a Deaf congregation. But in their place are hands choreographed in rhythm; bodies incarnating the many words of the liturgy; faces expressing the pain of crucifixion, the joy of resurrection, the peace of presence. Drama, mime, liturgical dance, and slides are some of the many visual art forms that enhance the worship of the congregation just as music enhances "hearing worship."

Understanding the many purposes of the Deaf church is integral to understanding the issues of justice that emerge in the context of preaching. The Deaf church is not simply the community that gathers for worship and the various ministries of the church. The Deaf church (like other linguistic minority churches) is one of the safe havens in the community where the language and culture of the community are preserved, celebrated, and passed down to future generations. Often not able to easily communicate in their various neighborhoods and jobs during the week, people who are deaf gather on Sunday mornings (and frequently stay for many, many hours!) not only for spiritual nurture but also for a true sense of community—a sense of acceptance and belonging. The Passing of the Peace may take as long as the sermon. When the community gathers, it is important for every person to greet every other person during this time.

When I was appointed pastor of a new Deaf congregation in Maryland, I was not fully prepared for what awaited me. Deaf preaching has some unique aspects that I discovered accidentally. Imagine my surprise when I first asked a rhetorical question in a sermon and four people in the congregation signed the answer back to me![4] I later learned that Deaf preaching has its own participatory, "call and response" form.[5] Deaf preachers often build questions into their sermons designed to elicit a short response from members of the congregation. They may also use a variety of visual forms to aid them in the proclamation of the Word: drama, slides, newsprint, objects, and so forth.

THE ORAL/AURAL NATURE OF THE LANGUAGE OF PREACHING

Only in a few homiletical resources on creative preaching (such as Thomas Troeger's *Creating Fresh Images,* now out of print) will one find visual proclamation of the Word encouraged. For the most part it is assumed that preaching involves one person speaking (dialogic preaching is still considered the exception, not the norm) while many listen. Underlying these basic assumptions about what is preaching and what is not lies a theology about who God is (One who *speaks* to individuals and *hears* their prayers); how God operates in the world (God *spoke* and the world came into being); how God became incarnate in the world as the *Word*; who we are in relationship to God (being made in God's image); and how we communicate with God (by *speaking* and *listening*). Based on this theology, speech and hearing have become essential elements for homiletics. This theology raises many justice issues for persons who are deaf in our churches today.

The language of homiletics is almost solely oral and aural. We talk about the preacher as the *speaker* and the congregation as the *hearers*. In litanies, the congregation often responds with "*hear* our prayer." The hymns we sing present images of "the *voice* of God is calling" and "open my *ears* that I may *hear*." How is it possible for people who cannot hear to feel at home in such an orally and aurally oriented context?

Luther made popular the Romans 10:17 text, "Faith comes by hearing," as well as the phrase that is currently reiterated by several homileticians, "Preaching is an acoustical affair."[6] According to Luther:

> God no longer requires the feet or the hands or any other member; [God] requires only the ears. . . . For if you ask a Christian what the work is by which he [or she] becomes worthy of the name "Christian," [that person] will be able to give absolutely no other answer than that it is the hearing of the Word of God, that is, faith. Therefore the ears alone are the organs of a Christian.[7]

The oral and written Word are the only means chosen and appointed by God to communicate with the human race till the end of the world.[8]

Theologically, if physical hearing through the ear is required for faith, persons who are deaf do not have access to God. Deaf people are then relegated to that "other" category—not totally animal or vegetable but not fully human either. I remember early on in my ministry at the Deaf church when I overheard a hearing person commenting on several of us signing together: "Look at them! All the grunts and gestures—it's like a bunch of animals." Deaf people who used sign language were historically compared to animals.

DOES FAITH COME FROM HEARING?

Sign language has received much more respect in recent years, but it has not been that long ago when deaf people hid their signs so they would not be perceived as less than human. The theology that equates physical hearing with faith denies deaf people access to faith, a personal relationship with God, participation within the Christian community, and the opportunity to respond as faithful disciples.

The theology that hearing is necessary for faith and a true relationship with God has become very prominent in homiletical circles. In *Homiletic*, David Buttrick states, "No wonder the Bible is big on words: God created with a Word, and we have faith by hearing."[9] In *As One Without Authority*, Fred Craddock says that the human "is a speaking animal. That people can speak and hear is their primary gift."[10] Walter Brueggemann, in *Finally Comes the Poet*, states that "it is speech and only speech that bonds God and human creatures."[11]

Given this tremendous emphasis on speaking and hearing in preaching, it is difficult for traditional preaching not to be oppressive to persons within the Deaf church. When the so-called experts preach that one's faith depends upon one's ability to *hear*, and being in relationship with God depends upon *speech*, the homiletical literature virtually denies the existence of the culturally Deaf within the Christian community. Justice seems light-years away, when deaf preachers will be treated as equal partners in the field of homiletics; when visual modes of preaching will be respected equally with aural modes; when sign language interpreters will be provided for deaf persons to receive a seminary education to become not only pastors but also professors; when the language we use to describe preaching will move away from strictly oral and aural images.

WHO PROFANES THE SANCTUARY?

This "less than human" attitude of many hearing people toward deaf people has many ramifications. Deaf people are perceived as *not whole* and therefore not *holy* enough for the realm of the sacred — the worshiping community. Since they are missing an essential element for Christian faith — hearing — and often choose not to speak, their presence is not always welcomed within the human community. Within the *holy* community their presence is sometimes believed to be an affront to God. This idea has its roots in Leviticus 21:17–23, which denies persons with certain physical characteristics from approaching the altar. It follows shortly after the chapters in

Leviticus (13–15) that outline the purity codes—the things that are clean and unclean, acceptable and unacceptable, for the purpose of religious ritual and social interaction.

> Speak to Aaron and say: No one of your offspring throughout their generations who has a blemish may approach to offer the food of his God. For no one who has a blemish shall draw near, one who is blind or lame, or one who has a mutilated face or a limb too long, or one who has a broken foot or a broken hand, or a hunchback, or a dwarf, or a man with a blemish in his eyes or an itching disease or scabs or crushed testicles. No descendants of Aaron the priest who has a blemish shall come near to offer [God's] offerings by fire; since he has a blemish, he shall not come near to offer the food of his God. He may eat the food of his God, of the most holy as well as of the holy. But he shall not come near the curtain or approach the altar, because he has a blemish, that he may not profane my sanctuaries; for I am [God]; I sanctify them. (Lev. 21:17–23)

Although deafness is not specifically mentioned here, it has been assumed that deafness is a "blemish" sufficient enough to *profane* the sanctuary. Historically, this text was used selectively to deny ordination to persons with certain disabilities. It was applied to those who were blind, lame, or disfigured in any way, yet it was not applied to the thousands of us who have had a "broken foot" or "broken hand" (v. 19), a "blemish" in the eyes (v. 20), or any rash that might be called "an itching disease" (v. 20).

Why was this text used selectively to discriminate against some but not others included in the text? Some would argue that blindness, lameness, and disfigurement are permanent disabilities while the others are more temporary. Others argue that those who are blind, lame, or disfigured are fewer in number, which means the larger majority are not excluded. I believe it has to do with the Gospel healing miracle narratives, which disabilities are included, which are not, which are associated with punishment from sin, and which ones Jesus cures. The three disabilities listed in the Leviticus text that have traditionally been excluded from the priesthood and ordination are all found in the Gospel healing miracle narratives. The others are not (unless an "itching disease" is associated with leprosy, in which case persons with leprosy—Hansen's disease—are likewise excluded from the ordained ministry).

Mark 2:1–12 explicitly equates the man's paralysis with sin, and several other texts have been interpreted over the centuries in a similar fashion: sin caused the disability and faith will cure it. This association with disability and sin, or disability and lack of faith, causes persons with disabilities to be unworthy to be ordained. There is also the notion that the minister stands in place of Christ. It was the argument used against the ordination of women—that women could not *re-present* Jesus and therefore could not be ministers. Some believe that persons who are blind, lame, or disfigured cannot *re-present* Jesus, who was perfect. The belief that certain physical characteristics can profane the holiness of the sanctuary is still in existence today. It also contributes to secular society's belief that persons who cannot hear or people with other disabilities are not worthy enough to be equal participants in the human community.

Deaf persons within the Deaf culture face such attitudes as they encounter a wide variety of injustices in our society. Perceptions of deaf persons as *not whole* and *less than human*, combined with misunderstandings about the complexity of American Sign Language, often result in the assumption that deaf people have a diminished intellectual capacity as well as their deafness, which leads to underemployment and unemployment. When communicating with someone through an interpreter, the hearing person often looks at and talks to the interpreter rather than the deaf person, as if the deaf person did not exist. Within society, it is assumed that deaf persons will be a drain on society—not contributors to society. Within the church, the same assumption is made. It will be a ministry *to* persons who are deaf rather than looking forward to the contributions deaf people, will make to the life and ministry of the congregation.

Our theology of what constitutes the image of God, combined with an attitude of superiority on the part of hearing folk, contributes to the second-class status deaf people experience. Our homiletical language only supports this oppressive attitude that how deaf people live in the world is somehow outside the range of acceptable Christian experience. This *acceptable* Christian experience has been taught to us over the centuries in sermons that interpret a variety of texts in almost totally oral and aural language.

Until we can encounter the face of God in deaf persons, until we can preach that faith comes in a multitude of ways other than hearing, until we seek out the gifts and contributions deaf people make to the Christian experience, until we stop calling the people sitting in the pews the "hearers," until our language and attitudes change, deaf people will always be on the periphery of the Christian community, and Deaf preaching will be relegated to the outer margins, given the norm that has been established by the homiletical profession.

PREACHING JUSTICE AMONG PERSONS WITH DISABILITIES

Preaching justice among persons with various disabilities also involves the language we use that can be either welcoming and accepting or alienating and judgmental. The language issue here involves more how we articulate our theology and how we interpret the various biblical texts rather than the language we use about the preaching act in general.

HEALING VERSUS CURE

One language issue that concerns people with various disabilities is use of the terms "healing" and "cure." Often we use "healing" when we really mean "cure": "Jesus *healed* Bartimaeus." In reality, these words can mean very different things. "Healing" evokes images of well-being and a sense of peace in mind and spirit, as in "healing presence," "healing moment," or "healing service." "Cure," in contrast, implies an elimination of not only physical *symptoms* but their *causes* as well.

A healing service may hope, even pray, for a cure for a particular individual; however, the intent of the service is to bring a sense of well-being into the person's life, a sense of comfort, support, and peace. Although some diseases may be cured through medical science, or even in spite of medical science, many disabilities are incurable. Rev. Harold Wilke,[12] who was born without any arms, will not suddenly grow them back no matter how many people pray for him. Persons who live with quadriplegia will not "leap, ye lame, for joy."[13] Most persons who are born blind will not see; nevertheless, they can experience healing in their lives.

This is not to deny that miraculous cures can happen, but to be realistic in helping people live with their disabilities. The focus of healing services should be on *healing*, not cure. When *cure* becomes the goal of the pastor or the congregation, the persons with the disabilities often do not feel accepted *as they are*. The implications are that only when they are *cured—*fully whole—will they be acceptable to the worshiping community. This attitude goes back to the Leviticus laws of purity and impurity—what is holy and unholy, what is acceptable to God and what profanes the sanctuary (Lev. 13–15).

But other factors are operating as well. People with disabilities are constant reminders of one's vulnerability and mortality. Many people cannot imagine a life without sight or hearing or the ability to take a walk on the beach. I have heard people say, "There but for the grace of God go I," when they look at someone who became paralyzed from a diving accident. The underlying assumption here is that God's grace was not present for the person who now lives life from a wheelchair.

A friend who recently celebrated her sixty-third birthday told me that God has "blessed" her with good health. It is true. She is in great health and has lots of physical and mental energy for whatever tasks she undertakes. But the corresponding belief to that statement is that I am somehow cursed by God because my health at a much younger age is fraught with episodes of severe muscle weakness and paralysis.

These unstated, underlying beliefs make it difficult for persons with disabilities to feel accepted *as they are* in many faith communities today. Their presence in worshiping congregations makes many people feel uncomfortable for many reasons. Though the Christian message involves "taking up one's cross," there is still an underlying belief that being a Christian entitles one to God's blessings and abundance. Living with a disability is not perceived to be one of God's blessings. Cure, then, becomes a way of accepting persons into full community within the life of the church. Cure is proof of God's blessing; the curse is removed. Persons who do not experience a cure, however, feel unacceptable because of the very nature of their existence.

Healing versus cure also becomes an issue when we preach the Gospel miracle stories. In the stories where Jesus cures someone, we call them healing narratives. We preach how Jesus can heal our lives as well, but "cure" is implied as the underlying definition of "heal."[14] These Gospel miracle narratives raise at least two other justice issues for preachers:

1. What do we believe theologically about persons with disabilities in the text and persons with disabilities today?
2. What homiletic do we employ in preaching these texts?

THE ROLE OF GOD

The question about God's relationship with persons with disabilities stems from a popular Christian belief that diseases, illnesses, and particularly disabilities are somehow part of God's will or overall plan. In an attempt to make sense out of suffering, people use a variety of explanations to attribute disability to God's will. Some people believe that disability is a punishment from God for some sin caused by the person. Consider the condemnation upon gay men who have contracted AIDS. Unfortunately, too many still today believe that God is punishing the person for his sexual orientation by *giving* him AIDS.

Others believe that disability is a punishment from God for one's parents' sin. At a conference I met a clergywoman whose daughter was recently diagnosed as profoundly deaf. The clergywoman's neighbor was a conservative Christian who believed the ordination of women was the work of the devil. Upon learning of the daughter's deafness, she told the clergywoman, "God is punishing you for being ordained." The disability of the daughter was attributed to the perceived sin of the mother.

Some people believe that disability is God's way of testing the person's faith. Several people have said to me that they were confident I would "pass this test" with flying colors and be back to normal again soon. What does this mean? That if I still have episodes of paralysis, I have failed the test? Is cure the only sign of God's full blessing?

For other people, God's purpose in causing or allowing a disability is to teach the person particular lessons: patience, humility, interdependence. People have commented to me that because of my disability, God has taught me discipline, how to work well in advance of due dates and how to be extremely focused since I never know what tomorrow will bring. But did God *give* me the disability in order to learn these things?

Some people acknowledge their uncertainty about why their disability is part of God's will, yet they believe strongly in some unknown divine reason—some divine plan. But how do we reconcile God's will with a baby born with multiple disabilities or a former chief executive officer with Alzheimer's disease? What sin of an innocent infant is being punished or what lessons could possibly be learned when one cannot remember what was served for lunch?

Many persons who live with a disability believe that God uses them in the midst of their disability to reach out to others, to be in ministry with others. I can learn many things living with my disability. However, the question is, Did God cause the disability *in order for* this ministry to happen or these lessons to be learned, or does God resurrect the various situations in our lives, fill us with grace, and help us make meaning out of our disability without God's causing or allowing it? Can we believe in a God who is not in control of every area of our lives? Can we find meaning in the midst of suffering without believing that it is somehow part of God's divine plan? Can we pray for healing while being realistic that a cure is highly improbable, if not impossible?

If disabilities are not caused by God, what can we as communities of faith believe that reconciles the reality of disability with a loving, compassionate God? To begin with, the notion of an all-powerful God needs to be challenged. Many people believe that God is indeed controlling everything that happens in the world. God determines natural disasters and personal crises—or at least God has chosen not to stop them. God, then, is responsible for wars, hurricanes, nuclear accidents, rape, the hole in the ozone layer, homelessness, famine, child abuse, toxic-waste dumps, and earthquakes as well as disability.

INTERDEPENDENCY

Often the choices of human beings are responsible for the situations we are in. The world is so interconnected and interdependent that what we do affects the lives of others and the earth itself. All matter is interrelated. A person's genetic DNA is directly related to her or his parents' genes and their parents' genes, and sometimes the combinations create the condition where disability will be the result. Sometimes matter is affected by other matter and mutations occur. The human immunodeficiency virus (HIV) is a living organism vying for control in the context of other living organisms. A man forty-five years ago decided to earn a living by turning his land into a toxic-waste dump that contaminated the pond at a Girl Scout camp. The result is a variety of disabilities and illnesses. All of life is interdependent. That is very clear in the global universe in which we live.

But in the midst of it all, we are confident that God wills our well-being. The Christian tradition is one of resurrection. In the midst of suffering and even death, God can bring about transformation. Well-being, however, is different for each person. What one considers devastating and tragic may be the norm for another. We tend to place our values of well-being onto others.

When we think of persons who are deaf and blind, our minds conjure up the image of persons so deprived that their lives must exist in a permanently disvalued state, full of suffering and loneliness. They cannot see the rays of sun peeking through the clouds or snow gracing the needles of a pine tree, or hear the ocean through a conch shell or a child's shrill of delight. But who is to say that we are not missing just as much because we are not aware of the nuances in the vibrations felt during a jazz concert, or the direction we are walking toward based on which side of our body is sunward and which is in the cool of the shadows, or the emotions evoked based on the texture of the bronze, the curve of the cut, and the depths of the grooves that etch an expression in the face of a sculpture. God takes the lives that we have and provides transforming opportunities for us as we strive toward well-being.

These transforming opportunities may come through someone's comforting touch, the loving acceptance of another, a hug, or an invitation to a meal. Through faithful communion with others—true community—we experience the loving presence of God. We work interdependently with God to achieve well-being for ourselves and others. We are agents of God in bringing about transformation in the lives of others. The preaching act is one aspect of ministry that offers us an opportunity to affirm the living reality of persons with various disabilities. As preachers preach justice, God is not the culprit to be blamed for the disability. Instead, God is the source of the many resurrections and transformations in our lives that allow us to live with the disability with grace and dignity.

In the Christian community we use language such as "family of God," "communion of the saints," and "the body of Christ." This foundation of our faith identifies us as a people who are interdependent upon one another (past and present) and upon God. We take care of one another, not only in times of crisis, but on a regular basis as well. The church as the family of God means that we are there for one another and, we hope, for the world.

The community of believers and the love of God support us in our journey of life, the joys and the trials: "If one member suffers, all suffer together with it; if one member is honored, all rejoice together with it" (1 Cor. 12:26). Our Christian tradition is based on community and our interdependence upon God and one another. What we model in our worship leadership and who has access to the pulpit can live out this sense of true community, or it can proclaim the message that only a select few are worthy. When a person who is blind reads the Scripture text from Braille, a person with Down's syndrome serves communion, or someone with paraplegia preaches from a wheelchair, the face of God is encountered in the midst of this interdependent community.

American culture does not always value interdependence, however. It places a high value on *in*dependence. Many in the United States are raised to believe that the American Dream is possible if we just "pull ourselves up by our own bootstraps." These and like messages shape public opinion, encouraging the value of independence as something toward which we must strive.

Dependency is perceived as something to be avoided. To be dependent is to be weak. It is tolerable for children and persons in the last years of life, but for anyone between the ages of eighteen and seventy, dependence is questionable. One must have a good reason to be dependent in these so-called productive years of life. Many persons with disabilities fall within this category. The reality is that most persons with disabilities are dependent upon someone or something at various times in their lives.

The church is called to be the place where people can be accepted for who they are as children of God, the place where dependency is acknowledged and interdependency is valued. A theology of interdependence honors the value of all individuals not by what they do, but by who they are, recognizing that all persons contribute to the community by their being, not by their doing. Interdependence acknowledges not only our dependence on God and one another, but also God's dependence on us to be agents of God's healing compassion in the world. It recognizes that all living organisms in the universe are connected and vying for life.

THEOLOGICAL CONCERNS

Knowing what one believes theologically on these issues is crucial to preaching justice. If a woman becomes paralyzed from the neck down because a drunk driver smashed into her car, what comfort is it when the preacher implies that it is God's will? If sin is the cause, should not the drunk driver be the one paralyzed? Was all this suffering necessary for a lesson or two to be learned, and how does one know what lesson is to be learned or whether one has learned it or not? Certainly, the paralysis does not go away once the lesson has been learned. So what are we preaching theologically when we imply that disability is caused by God or is the will of God?

The same issue arises when we are faced with deciding how to preach any one of the many Gospel miracle narratives that deal with Jesus' curing someone. If we believe theologically that God causes disabilities in order to test one's faith, then these Gospel texts are often preached with *faith* as the primary theme—the faith of the person with the disability in the text was the prerequisite foundation for the cure. Faith is often a major topic in sermons on these texts.

But according to the text, nothing indicates that the man who was deaf and whose speech was incomprehensible (Mark 7:31–37) even knew who Jesus was, let alone had *faith* in him. In the long pericope in John 9, the man who was born blind came to faith *after* Jesus cured him of his blindness—not before. And in Mark 2:1–12, Jesus made it clear that the faith of the *friends*, not of the man who was paralyzed, inspired Jesus. In the story of the woman with the hemorrhage (Mark 5:25–34), Jesus did not even know what was happening to him. The cure happened before he knew of the woman's desperation. Yet today, too often these texts are preached that faith is a necessary requirement *before* "healing" — meaning cure — can take place.

A friend's son lived courageously with a form of epilepsy that was not able to be totally controlled even with medication. He started going to a church that preached faith as the only prerequisite for being cured. Obviously since Sig still had epilepsy, he did not have faith — at least he did not have enough of it, or he did not have a deep enough faith (whatever that means) or his epilepsy would be gone. Trying to prove his faith, Sig stopped taking his medication. Several days later, he had a severe seizure and died at the age of twenty-three.

What word of healing are we conveying when we preach that faith will cure the various diseases and disabilities we live with? And does not that message also imply that lack of faith causes bad things to happen to good people? But we know that many good, faithful people in this world continue to live with disabilities, and we also know that a lot of faithless people with little regard for human life live very healthy lives.

The connection between faith and cure just does not make sense in the real world. This is not to deny that faith is an extremely important aspect in the lives of persons with various disabilities. Often their faith keeps them going in the midst of the many injustices they face in society and in the church. Faith brings *healing* to their lives — a sense of well-being in the midst of disability. Faith helps people *live* with their disabilities.

But let's face it, no amount of faith will bring back the legs of a veteran that were amputated as a result of injury during a war. And faith as a necessary condition for cure tends to be the focus primarily for the diseases and disabilities included in the Bible: epilepsy, blindness, deafness, paralysis, leprosy. We would not even consider faith as an issue for a broken leg, the flu, diabetes, or heart problems. Where do we draw the line? When is faith necessary for a cure, and when is it not? To continue to preach first-century medical views in today's technological world seems ludicrous at best.

METAPHORICAL INTERPRETATIONS

Many preachers, however, do not believe the theology that disability is a result of one's sin or a test of one's faith or that sufficient faith is the sole or primary cause of one's cure. Still these texts appear in the lectionary or a preacher feels called to address one of these Gospel narratives. In an attempt to deal with these texts justly, these texts are preached metaphorically: "We are all *blind* to the will of God."

There is great support for this approach because the Gospel writers themselves tend to use these texts to deal with much more than a particular individual with a disability. Mark, especially, uses these texts to show how the disciples were *blind* and *deaf* to who Jesus was. The members of a congregation, then, become the contemporary disciples who are likewise *blind* and *deaf* to God's commands.

The problem with this metaphorical interpretation is that the physical disability of a few is equated with the sins of many! In the biblical text, however, Jesus does not raise Bartimaeus up as an example of sin; the man born blind, the woman with the hemorrhage, and the ten persons with leprosy are not used in this way either. Yet somehow we take the physical condition and make it a reference for sinful behaviors. The result is that while theologically we are not preaching that the disability is the *result* of one's sin, we are now saying that the physical condition itself implies sin — that the very condition is a sign of sin.

In religious vocabulary, blindness and deafness are always used in negative ways to describe some condition of sin, some broken relationship with God: "You can be blind in a pew, and deaf in front of an altar";[15] "It is the blindness of humankind who praises the miracle worker . . . but wants nothing to do with his cross";[16] "People are too deaf to catch the sobs of grief . . . too hard of hearing to catch the rumble of discontent over injustice."[17]

Preaching the Gospel miracle texts that focus on "cure by faith" identifies persons who live with a disability as *faithless* — living in some sin, some broken relationship with God. But preaching these texts metaphorically also equates disability with sin. It is not the person who is faithless but the disability itself that is identified with sin. It is true that some preachers precede their metaphorical usage of disability language with the term "spiritual," as in "spiritual blindness" or "spiritual deafness." The argument is that the term "spiritual" implies that the blindness and deafness are not physical attributes but clearly metaphorical. The result is the same, however. Blindness and deafness are still equated with sin.

Both approaches to preaching these texts also imply that disability is something that a person *chooses*. Preaching faith as the answer to disability assumes that the persons *choose* not to believe strongly enough or deeply enough, because if they did, they would be cured. Preaching these texts metaphorically, being "blind to the will of God" or "too deaf to catch the sobs of grief," implies that people *choose* to disobey God and *choose* to ignore the cries of injustice.

But disability is not a choice people make, and the use of sensory language in the pulpit influences society's attitudes toward persons with disabilities. Disability is a part of everyday existence for millions of people and their loved ones in this world. Persons with disabilities are found in most congregations in the United States.

PREACHING JUSTICE: AN IMAGE

We can preach justice by carefully considering how we interpret the biblical texts that deal with someone being cured from a disability. We can choose language for our sermons and worship liturgies that does not equate disabilities with sin. We can proclaim a God who does not cause disabilities but is able to transform our lives in the midst of them. We can help people encounter the face of God in someone maneuvering a wheelchair with an elbow or giving a lecture in sign language. We have a choice whether to preach justice in ways that bring healing into the lives of persons with disabilities or to preach in a way that reinforces oppression and misunderstanding. Justice will come when preaching is imaged as signing hands and animated bodies and when the perceived "broken bodies" of individuals are accepted in the holy sanctuary where the body of Christ is broken.

CHAPTER TWO

A Native American Perspective

"THAT THE PEOPLE MAY LIVE"

MARTIN BROKENLEG

A S AN ACT OF MINISTRY, preaching in Native American communities naturally comes from elders. At her fifty-seventh wedding anniversary feast, eighty-year-old Nellie Two Hawk exhorted the community when she said, "In our married life, sometimes even love goes away but the vows of commitment we make will last all of our lives." She understood and used the power of the spoken word. This is a significant power in cultures that are still mainly oral ones.

As an ordained Episcopal priest, I understand preaching as a major vehicle accomplishing the task of religion, *re-ligio* in Latin meaning "to reconnect persons with the sacred and with one another." Preaching as an act of ministry is the act of making all persons relatives of God and kinsfolk of one another. I believe preaching accomplishes this task by stirring the conscience of the listeners, inspiring true thoughts, healing wounded hearts, and bringing listeners into full involvement with the sacred.

I am writing out of a lifelong experience of maturing in Lakota (Sioux) culture, with my childhood home being on the Rosebud Reservation in south central South Dakota. I have been a priest in the Episcopal Church for twenty-six years; I serve as canon at the local Episcopal cathedral and work on theological education for my diocese. I am a tutor for the Master of Divinity by Extension, a Native Ministries program of the Vancouver School of Theology in British Columbia. I am an oblate of Blue Cloud Abbey, a Roman Catholic Benedictine men's community in northeast South Dakota. For the past twenty-two years I have been a professor at Augustana College in Sioux Falls, South Dakota. Although my education is in theology and psychology, I am a full professor teaching Native American studies. I also work as a therapist and have a small private practice. I am a traditional Lakota dancer and have studied the Lakota cultural tradition, as is necessary for this role. My main preaching location currently is the predominantly urban Lakota community of *Tiospaye Wakan* (the Sacred Family) at the Episcopal cathedral in Sioux Falls.

SOCIAL LOCATION

Presenting this discussion as coming from the voice of all Native Americans would be misleading. The concept of "Native Americans" is not a reality. The hundreds of distinctive peoples native to North America have nothing in common except for our experience with the immigration of European peoples and then with American society. Within fifty years of first contact with European immigrants, hundreds of Native communities along the Atlantic seaboard died of previously unknown diseases. By 1890 the Native population of North America had fallen from approximately twenty million to a few hundred thousand. Many Native peoples no longer exist. The peoples who have survived have cultural or religious similarity due only to our common experience with America.[1]

Various terms will be used to speak of Native Americans: "aboriginal people," "First Nations people," "Native people," or simply "The People," the name most Native peoples call ourselves. Usually, the specific nation should be identified, such as Dine or Cheyenne. Doing this would be awkward, however, so the generic designation of "Native people" will be used most frequently when speaking of the people native to this continent. "Lakota" will be used for my nation.

This discussion will be from a Lakota perspective. The usual governmental term for the Lakota Nation is "Sioux." The Lakota people are scattered on reservations across Nebraska, Minnesota, South and North Dakota, Montana, and the Canadian provinces of Manitoba and Saskatchewan. Many more Lakota have migrated to cities all across North America. Taken as an entire people not divided by international borders, the Lakota people are probably the largest Native community on the continent and so are representative of a Native voice.

The image of Native Americans has been shaped by American history, philosophy, legislation, entertainment, and advertising. The common national myth of Native people is nearly identical to the life and culture of the Lakota. This image of "the Indian" was popularized by movies as late as *Dances with Wolves*. Interwoven with the image of "the Indian" was the image of a dying race. Native people were understood to be victims of the building of the United States and of inevitable progress. The imagined nomadic lifestyle was characteristic of very few Native peoples, brief in duration, and recent for even the Lakota. The Lakota, during this more recent era, are characterized by a nomadic life living in tipis, riding horseback, and following the buffalo. As the people most like the national myth of "Indians," the Lakota are a reasonable choice for a Native voice in preaching.[2]

This discussion is from the perspective of the Lakota (Sioux) Nation located in South Dakota. South Dakota has eight reservations, but unlike every other state, all the reservations are populated by the people of one nation: the Lakota. In the late 1990s the Lakota population in South Dakota is greater than sixty thousand.

HISTORICAL FACTORS

Native people associate the coming of emigrants from Europe and elsewhere with a resulting experience of population, military, cultural, and spiritual loss. Diseases from Europe decimated Native populations. More than three hundred years of military conflict eventually resulted in the defeat of Native peoples and removal from our ancestral homelands. Removal is the forced relocation to reservations. Leaving an ancestral land base and way of life brought rapid, repugnant, and radical cultural changes to the Lakota as to every other aboriginal people in North America. The material culture of European peoples was admired and mainly welcomed by Native communities, even though a dependency on those commodities weakened the political power of some Native Americans. Concomitant with those changes came a vast body of law including the treaty system. The profound changes in lifestyle drastically altered the spiritual ways that had been the basis of survival of First Nations peoples.[3]

Christianity entered the lives of Native people as an accomplice to the military, political, and cultural forces. Those forces irrevocably altered life as previously known on this continent. Missionaries came with soldiers and government officials. The message of Jesus faded against the blast of cultural change. For Native young people, indoctrination and psychological abuse in schools included memorizing catechisms and kneeling in church. Massacres of entire Native communities stained the Christian reputation of the soldiers and officers. The Christian faith, as introduced to Native people, is not clean.

The Quaker plan was federal policy from 1874 to 1890. The plan resulted from the Quaker appeal to the president to bring order to the interdenominational competition of the missionaries for Native souls. The plan officially assigned each Native nation to a Christian denomination for missionary effort. So, the Nez Perce were assigned to the Presbyterians. The Crow were eventually assigned to the Baptists. The Lakota Nation was assigned to the Episcopal Church. Some Lakota communities in present-day Minnesota had already welcomed Congregational and Presbyterian missionaries, and they remained. At a later time some Lakota leaders asked to have Roman Catholic missionaries assigned because they were already known. As a result of that assignment, the Lakota had two denominations for an official assignment.[4]

The Episcopalians moved quickly to ordain a Native clergy. Ordination requirements for Catholic clergy seemed to be a barrier to seeking ordination for Lakota Catholics. In recent years a married Lakota diaconate has emerged with vigor in the Catholic Church. Naturally, both denominations translated their worship materials into the Lakota language. The Lakota in eastern South Dakota were evangelized by Benedictine priests and monks, Benedictine nuns, and Presentation sisters. The Lakota west of the Missouri River initially came to know Jesuit clergy and Benedictine nuns. The Episcopal Church relied on white clergy mainly from Atlantic coast states, Lakota priests, deacons, and catechists.

The three major American institutions present in the Lakota community were the federal agency, the educational establishment, which usually took the form of a boarding school, and the Christian church. A collusion frequently developed among the three institutions involved in consciously and unconsciously changing Native American culture and life. Many Lakota accepted the changes as necessary for survival in the new way of life, but many other Lakota became embittered and hostile to all three institutions.

The Christian church was not able to distinguish culture from Christianity in its work with Lakota people. This is partially understandable because the factor of culture is mostly unconscious for everyone. Still, missionaries of the time did not separate their cultural lifestyle from their espoused religious tenets. They made no distinction between what was European culture and what was a teaching of Christianity. The story is told of the elder who asked the missionary what he had to do to be baptized. The reply was, "Cut your hair." The Lakota was doubly puzzled since the stained glass window of the Last Supper clearly showed Jesus and the apostles with long hair. Although there is obvious irony in this story, other confusions of culture with religion are more difficult to identify because of their complexity. For example, early missionaries promoted the Western value of agricultural enterprise as a necessary foundation for living a Christian life. The amalgamation of Christianity with Western culture has been a persistent and ongoing problem for Native people wishing to participate in Christianity.

In more recent times government programs have attempted to bring Native peoples into the mainstream of U.S. society through various efforts. In 1924 Native Americans were made citizens of the United States. In 1934 the Indian Reorganization Act made tribes legal corporations with the right to some level of self-government. In the 1950s federal programs moved younger Native people, aged eighteen to thirty-five, into seven target cities of Chicago, Minneapolis and St. Paul, Dallas, Denver, Los Angeles, Oakland, and Seattle. All of those cities have large populations of Native people today. According to the Bureau of Indian Affairs, by the 1990s more than 85 percent of Native people in the country were living off their reservations and usually in large cities.

Urban life has provided opportunities for Native people to participate in American life more consciously. This participation is not wholehearted but selective. Native people typically choose to engage in aspects of American life that bring benefits but do not require a loss of Native identity or culture. In this respect, Native people are probably the only American minority resisting full participation in American society. Most ethnic minorities seem to desire full participation in American life, but Native people wish certain benefits of society without accepting the entire philosophical or ethical principles of public American culture such as individualism, competition, and free enterprise profit.

Native people have learned skills to survive in American life. These skills enable The People to interact with American institutions to their benefit. The skill of articulating cultural difference is one ability that has helped define Native culture more consciously and deliberately. Defending Native liberties and rights has been possible with an educated community. The long history of treaty making is the basis for the sovereign status of Native people today.[5]

City life also brought Native people together socially and politically. This intertribal alliance is called Pan-Indianism.[6] Pan-Indianism is the political fusion of Native people into a cohesive federation. All of this contact would not have been possible without the language of the majority of Europeans: English.

The distinctive history of Native people is based on a legal and cultural identity that precedes the existence of American society and the introduction of Christianity. A firm grasp of the contact history of Native people with America is necessary to understand the place of preaching in our community today.

A Unique Voice

Certain philosophical assumptions influence a Native voice. These assumptions lay the foundation of the preacher's thought world as well as the assumptions of the listeners.

KNOWLEDGE BELONGS TO THE COMMUNITY

First, all knowledge, like all material goods, belongs to the collective community. While Native culture respects the freedom of the individual, the experience of this freedom occurs within the context of a communal mentality. Life experience and the discovery of the means to survive have promoted the Native peoples' value of communality over the individual.

It is at this point that Native American values differ the most from Western values. Not only from the first experiences of life but also through the very last experiences of living this life, Native people know the intensity of belonging to one another, to our communities, and to our homeland.[7] Consequently, all information and thinking begins and ends with the assumption that we are a single unit when together and that we will end up together. For example, discussions of ethics will assume the highest good is the good of the community and not that of the individual. Values such as sharing, generosity, and loyalty are highly esteemed in that they promote the cohesion of the community. Naturally, appeals to individual belief or individual salvation have no attraction to Native listeners.

An effective Native preacher is more likely to conclude any consideration with an exhortation to the values of the Native community, such as helping the poor, the weak, and the elderly. A Native preacher will appeal to the Native ethical standards of sharing, of using just enough resources to survive, of treating others as your nearest kinfolk and relatives as though these are the teaching of the religious hero.

ORAL PROMISES OVER WRITTEN ONES

Second, North American Native cultures are oral societies. One's word and one's words are highly esteemed and have a reality distinctive to themselves. In Lakota society, the words one speaks are regarded as real aspects of the speaker. They are something from that person, just as one's blood or sweat is from that person. In this respect, words are respected as personal and valuable.

In traditional Lakota communities, barbers are known to sweep up the hair of a customer and give it to him as he leaves the barbershop. The spirit of the customer is in that hair; it belongs to him, and yet has an existence of its own. Just as we treat a person's hair with respect, as containing something of the person it comes from, so we respect the very words from a speaker. Somehow, the words contain the spirit of the speaker, and yet they have an existence independent of the one who spoke the words.[8] We quote the words of another person with accuracy and truth because it would be a personal injustice to misquote another's words or intention.

A preacher will be conscientious in citing the words of another and will expect to be corrected by an elder if an error is made. To be expected to speak at any occasion is considered an honor because it is an invitation to give of oneself. To give good words to others is an act of personal generosity, and Native people would recognize it as such.

To make clear an implication of this second aspect: for Lakota people, the spoken word has a power that the written word does not. If one is making an important point, as in promising to do something, it can be believed only when it is spoken. Moreover, what is stated in front of witnesses is considered a vow. An interesting point is that what is in writing has little value as far as Lakota culture goes. Something that is written down is made of little importance. For example, if my family were having a ceremony, and if we wanted certain people to be present, then we would invite them verbally in a face-to-face exchange. If we were to send a written invitation, our lack of spoken words would say that the gathering is of such small importance that we did not bother to put the invitation into words. The preacher, then, has accomplished something important since thoughts and affections have been put into words.

SPEAKING AND LISTENING

The third factor affecting a Native voice relates to Native cultures as oral cultures. In an oral culture, each person must possess high verbal intelligence and develop the best oratorical skills. In Lakota society, at every public gathering, hosts invite well-known speakers to address the gathering. Listening to speakers is a form of learning the ways of The People and providing entertainment as well as enlightenment. Naturally, listening skills are also expected. In historical times, Native children were educated in listening. At one time a five-year-old Lakota could hear one of the memories of The People that would take nearly two hours to hear and repeat what had been heard verbatim.[9]

Listening well requires an accurate memory, no side conversations, no eye contact with the speaker, and as little physical movement as possible since this is understood to convey respect for the speaker. From an early age Lakota young people are encouraged to speak at gatherings and to be prepared to speak when it is appropriate. While traveling to a gathering, Lakota parents tell the young people to prepare what they will say at the gathering and to be ready to say something encouraging to The People.

MULTIPLICITY

A fourth philosophical principle defining Lakota culture and guiding Lakota understanding is a definition of multiplicity. Western culture has a definition of singularity and moves toward that direction. Western governance systems used the principle of single (*monos* in Greek) origin (*arche* in Greek), the monarchy. Whether by election or evolution Western governance always assumes one leader. The principle of the singular is also found in Western notions of marriage (monogamy), religion (monotheism, even allowing for trinitarian definitions), creation (uni-verse), and singular conclusions. In contrast, Lakota thinking relies on the multiple. Governance is polyarchic with many "chiefs" in any community and no supreme chief. Marriage was mainly polygamous for Native peoples. The spirit world is populated by many spirits, but even this community is considered to be a united whole.[10] Native definitions of the world assume it is a multi-verse with many levels of existence. Conclusions may be multiple and can even consist of many factors that are in logical conflict.

This principle of multiplicity is so significant in Native thinking because it permits full participation in more than one entity without any conflict. It is perfectly possible to be a Lakota and to take full part in a Cheyenne ceremony. One would not be surprised to find a Navajo living fully in a Lakota community. In contemporary times it is possible for a Lakota to take part in our Pipe Religion and still be a full participant in a Christian church.[11] In fact the vast majority of Native people have a dual practice when it comes to religion. Native people would have neither logic nor allegiance problems with full participation in more than one religious system.

The complexity of this principle can be contemplated if one considers being fully involved in both a Roman Catholic and a Baptist church at the same time. All the conflicts that immediately arise in Western, singular-oriented thinking do not even occur in this Native, multiplicity-based understanding. As stated earlier, the wholehearted involvement of Native people in our Native religious system and in Christianity at the same time has major implications for preaching in our communities. Effective preachers rely on stories or principles from both systems to present teachings.

TRADITIONS AS GOD GIVEN

The fifth significant Native perspective involves our understandings of our way of life. Native Christians have theologized about the relationship of our traditional ways to Christianity.[12] Most Native communities view their spiritual and cultural traditions as God given. Among the Lakota we speak of the Lakol Wicoh'an, the Lakota way of life. That our way of life is God given is so essential that we have no word to distinguish religion from daily living. Our way of life consists of our memories of how the world came to be as it is, teachings of our understandings of how the world works, and the ceremonial traditions that make our understandings and meanings our reality. Everything—from common courtesies to complex religious actions—is a part of the Lakol Wicoh'an. Our mythology, basic education, and explanations of our arts and technology are all a part of this Lakota way of life.

Such a significant part of our lives cannot be taken lightly nor can it be discarded, as the early missionaries seemed to think necessary. To treat lightly the way of life revealed to us would constitute blasphemy. How, then, are we to theologize about the Lakol Wicoh'an other than as our own Old Testament? An Old Testament consists of the way of life God has revealed to a people. When the New Testament arrives, it can exist only on the foundation of the Old Testament. In our Old Testament we have the customs and teachings revealed to us by God, just as the Hebrew Scriptures contain the old ways revealed to the Jewish people by God. Their old ways cannot become the Lakota's ways. The Lakota's ways, the Lakol Wicoh'an, are the foundation onto which the teachings of Jesus are to be grafted. Reading the old ways of the Jewish people is instructive for us Lakota, but it cannot become our way of life. We use the Hebrew Scriptures to gain additional insight into the nature of the one God with whom both Jewish and Lakota people have a long-term relationship. These understandings frequently come from having very similar experiences and stories. The Lakol Wicoh'an is the Lakota way of life and the basis of our hearing of Jesus and Jesus' teachings.

Theologians refer to bringing together our way of living with the teachings of Jesus as "inculturation," the process by which the church takes on the symbols, materials, and the conceptual categories of a local population. Inculturation makes the teachings of Jesus incarnate in us as a people. Currently, the church is inculturated into Western European culture. The church's new task is to become inculturated to Native America.[13] This process requires using Native decorative arts, customs, and symbols in worship, and Native concepts for understanding the Savior.

For example, a preacher may use the image of a Lakota sun dancer who makes an offering of his suffering, "that The People may live," as an illustration of the significance of the crucifixion of Jesus. Still another preacher may use the self-giving of the elder from the former world in the form of a buffalo as a type of the way Jesus comes to us in Holy Communion. With inculturation, the faith comes to us as we really are in our situation as it really is.

RELIGION FOCUSES ON THIS LIFE

The sixth principle in a Native voice concerns the purpose of religion. Years ago a joke circulated that told of two young people observing an elderly woman who was reading the Bible. Asked why the grandmother was reading so diligently, one youth replied that she was studying for finals. The joke assumed, of course, that the purpose of Christianity is to achieve some standard, which then permits one into a life after this one. Probably most Native people would have found the joke confusing because Native religion's purpose is to live this life well. The teachings are to guide one into living life completely and appropriately. The ceremonies are to reenact and manifest the revelations and meanings that make living possible and necessary.

Many ceremonies mark events as sacred, which are defined as natural scientific processes in the West. For example, Native people typically welcome the first thunder as the change of season. The sacredness of that moment, that process, is the focus of the ceremony, however that is expressed. So also with marking the dawn. That moment is sacred, and so is rightly remembered by ceremonial observance. To live this life well, Native teaching says, one must know what is sacred, observe the way that has been established and revealed to us, and commit to live in that way as the Creator intended. Religion, in our understanding, makes survival possible.

Native teachings on women exemplify the connection of the sacred to survival. In virtually all of Native America, women are the more necessary sex in a community.[14] Typically, in Native mythologies, heroes are female. In Lakota mythology, our revealer, our messiah, is the White Buffalo Calf Woman. Many of our teachings and nearly all of our ceremonies are revealed by or through her. In many Native communities, women hold most, if not all, property. In numerous Native communities, people mark their ancestry by recounting their mothers. In Lakota society a woman is the most powerful during her menstrual cycle, her "moontime," since this is the sign that she can carry life. A woman is considered very powerful during this moontime because her sacred power is in her ability to carry life, give birth, and help The People survive. The sacred is given so that humanity can survive in this life well.

PREACHING JUSTICE

Four major topics are the focus of preaching justice in Native communities: gaining legal justice, understanding our cultural ways as God given, healing and spiritual wholeness, and divorcing Western culture from Christianity.

GAINING LEGAL JUSTICE

The first area is that of legal justice. The typical audience here would not be Native people but non-Native listeners who have interest in or obligation to observe legal requirements. The laws of the United States have much to say about the observance of treaties, the covenants made between sovereign nations. Because the existence and status of Native nations were prior to the existence of the United States, early covenants between the United States and Native nations were by treaty. Treaties have status in international law and are called by the U.S. Constitution "the supreme law of the land," indicating the seriousness of their obligation upon the United States. Because the United States does not observe even one of the nearly four hundred treaties it made with Native nations, a call to justice must include a call to observe Indian treaties. Although the international reputation of the United States is negatively affected by its nonobservance, seldom do preachers other than Native ones bring up this issue.

The Hebrew Scriptures create the image of Israel as possessing its land. That land was occupied by other peoples when the descendants of Abraham went there. What of those people? Was not the land in their possession?

Native Americans are more like the Canaanites than the people of Israel. During speeches on national holidays, Americans typically draw on the heroic image of creating a new promised land. For Native people, the same images are hollow or bitter. Perhaps more could be learned regarding just relationships between Natives and Newcomers by meditating on the fourteenth chapter of Genesis, the meeting of Abram (later to be Abraham) and Melchizedek, the local medicine man. In their encounter, they honor each other by giving what they have. Abram offers a tithe of the booty he carries with him; Melchizedek offers the fruit of the land where he had lived all along, bread and wine, the signs of the messianic presence. Should the United States meet its treaty obligations, Native America would surely see that time as messianic and a period of justice.

A related area of legal justice stands out for Native people who are now minorities in our own homelands. A minority is a social group that is defined as less than the dominant group.[15] While it may or may not be true that the minority is in fact less, the definition of being less persists. Minority status is not necessarily defined by race, although in American society racial difference does define one as less. Minority status is defined not by numbers but by low social and political status. Native Americans typically are both visually and economically invisible. Virtually all social indicators, including educational status, earning power, health care, life expectancy, and housing, show Native Americans as the least of all Americans. Other ethnic groups stand higher on social indicators. Consequently, the teachings of Jesus concerning care for the least in society give hope to Lakota and all other Native people. No fancy interpolation must be made from the scriptural mandates as far as Native people are concerned. God's care for the poor must surely mean God cares for Native people.

Probably every Native person can recount innumerable experiences with racism and discrimination. Whether it is children mocking media images of Native dances or school materials that consider Native people as museum tenants, racism persists. Even recent groups that claim to honor Native people, such as New Age religious followers, fall into racial stereotypes. They go to great lengths to find personal Native ancestry so that they can claim mystic knowledge. If they cannot find any Native ancestry in their history, then being a medicine man, or worse, a princess, in a former life will do. The underlying presumption is that Native spiritual knowledge is genetic and racial. Regardless of the form of racism, the promise of God is that justice will prevail, that we are loved by God, even if no one else can see us clearly.

UNDERSTANDING OUR CULTURAL WAYS

The second area for preaching justice to Native people is based on our understanding of our cultural ways. If God gives us our cultural ways, then we cannot disregard them. For a Lakota, knowledge of the Lakol Wicoh'an is integral to self-understanding. A true relationship with God is not possible if we do not know ourselves, for we are party to the relationship as much as God is. For a Native person, self-knowledge includes knowing the way of life we have been given. Yet this very knowledge was forbidden or suppressed for at least a generation. The experience of my parents during their years at a boarding school is typical of their generation. They found their language and ways of living denigrated and suppressed by teachers, administrators, and chaplains. For many Native people this suppression resulted in a loss of knowledge of what made them who they are. The absence of enculturation (not to be confused with inculturation, discussed earlier in this chapter), the process by which a child learns to function within his own culture, created a break in Native cultures. This break is not just a loss of some knowledge base, but it also creates an absence of internalized values. Without internalized values an individual is left to follow personal whim and appetite rather than function according to community standards. As a therapist, I have seen this dynamic more than once with Native American clients.

Still other losses can occur. When Native young people attended residential schools, they lost the living experience of their family wisdom. They did not see couples successfully resolve conflicts. They did not see parents successfully raise children. Most adults rely on this observed learning from experience for interpersonal situations. Native Americans who attended residential schools did not build this area of learning, and they frequently suffer problems in family living. Restoring the social and interpersonal skills from the cultural tradition can create a higher quality of life.

This building of the cultural tradition on the personal level is a task of justice, since the way of life has been given by the Creator. A preacher's role, then, would include defining and explaining the traditional way of life as a purpose for living. The preacher would explain the joys and obligations of being a Lakota in addition to being a Christian. Simply knowing that a cultural tradition exists often gives hope to Native people. Because that cultural tradition is theirs, Native people will have a greater allegiance to this culturally appropriate form of teaching. Restoration of the lost way of life for Native people is akin to the restoration of the people of Israel after the Babylonian exile. Turning to that period in the Hebrew Scriptures provides a model of wholeness for Native Christians.

HEALING AND SPIRITUAL WHOLENESS

Perhaps the greatest area of preaching for Native Christians lies in the realm of healing. From historic times, Native communities have defined health as a spiritual wholeness, and it is achieved through religious effort. Spiritual power has always been a healing power. For the past five hundred years Native people have known the brokenness that comes from suppression and destruction in all forms. Typically, Native participants in church life come with a variety of ills that need healing. Preaching justice would name the wounds, exorcise the evil forces that created the injury, and pronounce freedom and triumph through a relationship with the living God. The justice preacher addresses these ills and pronounces the healing that comes from God.

Recently, a significant church effort in Native communities has involved a dynamic called healing circles. In a communal setting, participants speak about their woundedness, and they receive encouragement from others. In one such setting I was asked to make the concluding remarks after participants spoke. My words were, "Get over it." I left a long pause. "Get over it because that is what God wants for you." The listeners were stunned by the opening, but then knew that they were not to get stuck on just naming their hurts without seeking the necessary healing. First Nations people have many wounds from the past. The word from God is that wholeness can be theirs for the asking and for the work involved. The preacher of justice advocates a transformation of social injustice and resistance to it in its many forms.

The most pervasive health issue for Native people is alcohol abuse.[16] Many Native persons have come to work recovery using the twelve step recovery programs. The designers of twelve step programs had their foundation in the spiritual healing tradition of the Christian church. Native people often find a solid recovery by working the twelve steps in conjunction with a revitalized learning of their tribal traditions.

Often called the Red Road approach, this healing relies on the person's allegiance to Native identity and the spiritual healing of twelve step programs based in Christian teachings. The principle of abstinence, for example, could be presented as a return to Native tradition since intoxicants were not produced or utilized among Native people in North America. The fifth step of admitting past wrongs to God and another person is a form of confession. It could be presented to a Native person as a cleansing, a familiar concept in nearly all Native cultures.

DIVORCING WESTERN CULTURE FROM CHRISTIANITY

Perhaps the biggest task for the preacher addressing Native American Christians is the task of divorcing Western culture from Christianity. In the entire history of Christian missions among First Nations people, seldom has a clear distinction been made between the teachings of Jesus and the tenets of Western culture. Since there was no distinction between culture and Christianity in the minds of early missionaries, that distinction is sometimes difficult for Native people to understand, let alone make with any certainty.

Numerous examples of this confusion can be cited. A Lakota elderly woman on hearing drum music in a eucharistic service was asked if she recognized the song. Her reply was that she was raised an Episcopalian. In another setting she would have known the song in all probability. Still another example comes from the altar guilds, which have care of the linens and altar cloths. Some contend that only items imported from England or from the East Coast are appropriate for church use. Perhaps the greatest chasm exists between Native persons who feel called to the ministry but who must first earn Western academic credentials to minister with any recognition. All of these examples show the necessity for some distinction to be made between the officiousness of the church and the Christian faith.

On at least one Lakota reservation the seminary-educated Lakota priest said that nothing Lakota should be used in the church. The result was a deep antagonism between younger Lakota people and the Christian faith. Since, in the past, becoming Christian meant sacrificing Lakota culture and identity, the call to live the faith in every culture must be spoken. This is not to say that culture supersedes the teachings of Jesus. Indeed, the teachings of Jesus are contrary to every culture, including American culture. Just as the teachings of Jesus correct some aspects of Lakota culture, so should they correct flaws in the culture of America.

The institution of the church has been an enemy of Native people, frequently causing a kind of cultural genocide as a requirement for being a Christian. For the faith to be seen clearly by Native listeners today, a clear distinction must be made between that former enemy and the faith of Jesus.

The Old Testament of Native peoples must be recognized as a clear foundation for the new life in Christ. In Lakota thinking, there is no such thing as original sin. One must preach from some other basis than the substitution theory of the crucifixion. In Lakota thinking there is no such thing as evil but simply the recognition that things just are. To begin to evangelize on the basis of needing Jesus to wipe away the condemnation of original sin would have no effect on any Native community.

The need for healing, both personal and communal, is strongly recognized by most Native people. That Jesus brings healing of both soul and body has a strong appeal to the experiences of contemporary First Nations people. There is a long-standing cultural basis for the healing tradition in nearly all Native cultures. Achieving wholeness so The People may live is a goal of all Native traditions. This aspect of the Christian faith, healing of body and soul, is the greatest asset of the church as far as Native Americans are concerned.

ONE URBAN NATIVE COMMUNITY

Tiospaye Wakan (the Sacred Family) is the urban Native Christian community in Sioux Falls, South Dakota. It is a portion of the total congregation of the Episcopal cathedral. Attendance varies greatly from 45 to 250, depending on the occasion, weather, and other factors. Native people usually make up 90 percent or more of the attendees. The average age is about twenty years old. Nearly all of those attending services are Lakota, but Crow, Hidatsa, Mandan, Ojibwa, Navajo, and members of other Native nations attend as well. Not all who attend are Episcopalian; some are Roman Catholic, United Church of Christ, Presbyterian, or Mennonite. Nearly two-thirds of the congregation are persons working some kind of recovery program, usually a twelve step program. All but one or two persons who attend are poor. Some live on the streets of Sioux Falls and rely on the local soup kitchen and shelters for their survival.

In preaching to this community there is little need to speak of the hardships in life. There is little value in preaching about the need to avoid sin. Many members of the congregation have endured tragedies all their lives. Many are resigned to lives of poverty and political disfranchisement.

The design of every successful sermon to this community relies on three elements. The first element is a lesson taken from the Gospels. Typically, an action of Jesus or his teaching will form the basis of the sermon. Frequently, some explanation of the teaching must be given. The second element of the sermon is a connection of the teaching to Lakota cultural tradition. Since many are not familiar with their cultural tradition, some teaching must be done to explain the tradition's origin and meaning. The third element of the sermon is the application of the teaching to living well, usually by touching on some aspect of the twelve step recovery programs.

The preacher briefly explores these three elements to set the background for the lesson in the sermon. The message of the sermon is best conveyed in a story familiar to the preacher or perhaps taken from Lakota mythology. In Lakota oratorical tradition, it is considered bad manners to explain the message. Once a story is told, it is left to the listener to interpret and apply the message. Consequently, the groundwork must be laid carefully before the story is told. If a story is told well, then it will speak to the heart, not to the mind only, but to the whole person. That is, it will be understood at a deep and wordless level. Almost never will there be any discussion or compliment to a well-composed homily. The sign the message has reached the heart is signaled by eyes moist with tears and nothing more.

This threefold foundation for preaching justice in my community has years of thought in it. The Gospel, the Lakol Wicoh'an, and the application to a survival model such as the twelve step program are all the groundwork for preaching to a contemporary Native American community.

CONCLUSION

Essentially, then, the major images used to preach justice in Native communities include the healing ministry of Jesus, the cultural traditions as Old Testament, and the love of God for those considered the least in the world. All of these images bring comfort and a deep truth to Native Christians.

Preaching as an act of ministry connects the lives of the listeners with the living God and teaches them that they are relatives to one another. Effective preaching in Native American communities requires that the preacher have some knowledge of history since the lives of present-day Native people have been heavily affected by the past. A preacher of justice for Native people will proclaim triumph over the dynamics of racism, cultural discrimination, broken treaties, and social injustices toward ethnic minorities. All of these social factors have a strong impact on the life of every contemporary Native person.

A loving preacher will connect Native people with our cultural traditions and through this unite us to the loving God. An appreciation for an inculturated Christianity will speak to Native people as our lives are. Native people have survived for untold centuries on this continent. We have a history of creative, successful cultures. We are a people who have also known captivity, defeat, and exile. We have seen our lands overtaken by other peoples. Like the people of Israel, we have longed for someone who would help us. We have found that in the medicine man Jesus. We believe he is one of us, the Native people, and that his closeness to the Creator has given him the teachings to a way of life that will help us survive.

CHAPTER THREE

An African American Woman's Perspective

RENOVATING SORROW'S KITCHEN

TERESA FRY BROWN

I AM AN AFRICAN AMERICAN WOMAN who is also an ordained elder in
the African Methodist Episcopal Church. Holding a doctor of philosophy in religion and social transformation and working as a professor of homiletics in a United Methodist seminary, I have had a faith journey filled with
valleys and mountains. I have found much meaning in these words of Zora
Neale Hurston: "I have been in sorrow's kitchen and licked out all the pots.
Then I have stood on the peaky mountain wrapped in rainbows with a harp
and a sword in my hands."[1] Preaching for the past fourteen years, I have had
access to places and opportunities that most of my preaching sisters have
not had. I have heard many songs from weary throats. At age eighteen I was
fascinated, frightened, and frustrated as I heard my first woman evangelist
preach, not from a pulpit but from the floor at a musical. I was a Black
Baptist living in Missouri, and women just did not do that kind of thing.
She was, according to my upbringing, surely going to hell. As my life developed, I joined her company by being the outcast, scorned and denied access to pulpits in many churches.

During my forty-six years, I have heard more than three thousand sermons, 90 percent of which were preached by Black men. That does not
include the number of sermons preached by my students over the past five
years or the approximately two hundred sermons I have preached. There are
still places, "sorrow's kitchens," where no preaching invitation will ever ma-
terialize or the pastor is being politically correct in inviting me to "speak" on
Women's Day or at a women's conference. There have been, however, "peaky
mountains" of affirmation where I have preached—some African Methodist
Episcopal, five Black Baptist, and some United Methodist churches.

THE PREACHING CONTEXT

The disheartening reality is that for most African American women preachers, there is a debilitating conflict between being under orders from God to preach from that weary throat and constantly hearing the voices of the brothers and sisters challenging one's authenticity. The hope for most women preachers is that the freedom of which they preach will come afterwhile. The struggle to preach is centuries old. The social issues are not new. The barriers change with each excuse for not ordaining women. The biblical texts give African American women songs in weary throats and a few guarantees that "afterwhile and by-and-by" we will all be free to praise and serve God as we see fit.

What are the social-political-cultural contradictions present in the Black church concerning women preaching? Is there historical evidence of Black women preaching in Black churches? If justice means having equal access to God's benefits, why is there resistance from many Black men and Black women to Black women receiving these benefits? How do Black women preachers deconstruct, reconstruct, and use the biblical text and contemporary society in the preaching event? What are examples of justice metaphors, images, and illustrations used by Black women in sermons?

The Black church is not a monolithic institution. There are as many names, belief systems, pastors, congregations, and hermeneutics as there are in any culture. Rooted in the cultural imperative that all must be free, the Black church began in the woods, swamps, caves, and secret places of institutional slavery in the early centuries of the Americas. The continuing struggle for a space to worship a God who affirmed their personhood and the dominion of all creation led to protests, walkouts, and "stealing away to Jesus." The Black preacher became the leader, social activist, counselor, and economic liaison for the Black community. The "man of God" had the right connections, and even slave owners and later segregationists diplomatically dealt with the Black preacher. The Black church was ascribed by voices within the Black community as the "cradle of freedom," "womb of education," and/or "social center for the community." The difficulty arose when those who made up the institution began their own form of oppression of another group within its walls that might not fit the model. As Black women voiced their "call" to a preaching ministry, the church officials closed ranks and adopted the motto "Just say no!" The cognitive dissonance of proclaiming freedom for all, yet continuing to enslave some, is curious. The answers are not easy or even available in some cases. There are, of course, those who affirm women preaching because of their belief that

God is the one who chooses and calls persons to preach. Still others have swept out pulpits, refused admission to women, banned women preachers from churches, and charged them with being "rebellious," "un-Christian," "home wreckers," and "subversive speakers." And these are the nice terms!

It has been my experience that the Black church has proved, at its best, to be an open, affirming entity with room enough for any and everybody. It is also, at its worst, an oppressive place for many persons, particularly for those who do not fit the social or gender-based roles determined by the culture or adopted from the wider culture. The role of women in many Black churches has traditionally been to sing in choirs, teach children, serve the pastor, give financial support, and keep the building clean. The pulpit is generally the venue of men. At its worst, the Black church repeats the exclusivity of the white churches before the independent Black church movement of the late 1700s. At its best, the Black church is the healing and nurturing place of many Black communities.

The Black church may be "sorrow's kitchen," or it may be the "peaky mountain" with the rainbows, harp, and sword. The peaky mountain is the place where God who is "no respecter of persons" resides and where African American women may "sit at the welcome table" with African American men. A mountain is where we all share in the "peace that passes all understanding" and where all of God's children decide their own paths and breathe air that is devoid of stinging epithets. It is also the place where faith communities in particular and U.S. society in general no longer treat Black women as ignorant, long-suffering baby factories with aberrant body images or appearances, who do not know what or in whom they believe. On the mountain faith, exuberance, freedom, community, and justice are available to all persons. Here Black women raise the sword of truth, which is the Word of God, for the entire community. This "peaky mountain" is the location of Black women singing God's praises unafraid and unashamed of the results. In faithfulness to a call from God these women—ordained and nonordained—"break the bread of life" for the freedom and salvation of the whole body.

"Sorrow's kitchen" must be renovated within any church and within any society that would oppress any segment of the community. The ideology and praxis of freedom and liberation of the Black church must be reestablished. Katie G. Cannon, African American womanist ethicist and ordained Presbyterian minister, states that the task of the liberationist is "debunking, unmasking, and disentangling the messages in African American sacred rhetoric."[2] African American preaching women who find their voice and publicly articulate their belief systems risk rejection and at times abuse. There is work to be done to expose the oppression by the Black church and Black male, and at times female, ministers and congregants. There must be an analysis of the cultural hermeneutics that allows one segment of the population to say a word for God, yet bars another from "standing in John's shoes." Recognizing the legacy, struggles, and victories of those preaching women who stood regardless of the social obstacles is essential to establishing the possibilities for transformation in the culture. If the African American faith community bases its existence on freedom, reconciliation, justice, and grace, the challenge is to unearth and reform the rules that would keep some imprisoned and others holding the keys.

Speaking of Renovation

Sociologist and ordained Baptist minister Cheryl Townsend Gilkes reviews the sociocultural issues of the Black church and Black preaching:

> The African imagination, in its criticism of white oppression, valued the vivid depictions of liberation within the Hebrew Scriptures and their New Testament connections. The Afro-American religious imagination is a biblical imagination. Generations of black Christians who endured slavery, reconstruction, Jim (Jane) Crow, urban migration, and the civil rights era constructed and fashioned their songs, prayers, testimonies and sermons with the English (King James Version) Bible as a resource for the interpretation of past and present sequences and events and for the envisioning of futures and of strategies to achieve those futures. The suggestion that black people and their preachers do religion with the Bible in one hand and the newspaper in the other reflects this tradition.[3]

Belief in God did not begin when the enslaved were "Christianized" by plantation preachers. There was an established belief of God in everything. The endurance of many enslaved persons under the brutal systems of chattel slavery was supported by the community belief that "God would make a way somehow"; that God, not the ones who controlled their physical lives, made the physical world; that the God they heard preached on special days was more than the God the plantation preachers proclaimed, "Slaves, obey your masters"; that the God they were drawn to made the waters, the air, the earth, and even their children, who would soon be sold away from them. Many were killed trying to learn to read the King

James Version of the Bible. They wanted to know the other parts of the story. Songs were developed, which served as messages about God and of the run toward freedom. Prayers were uttered that spoke of a forgiving and merciful God. Testimonies were raised that spoke of what God had done in the midst of their troubles. Black preachers began to speak a word to the enslaved that gave them hope for freedom in spite of what the "approved" preachers said about them. Sermons were composed with an eye for both the biblical text and the realities of the lives of the people. The relevance of the biblical text is supported by the actions of God in the lives of the people.

Paired with Amos 5:24 ("But let justice roll down like waters, and righteousness like an everflowing stream"), Luke 4:18 ("The Spirit of [God] is upon me, because he has anointed me to bring good news to the poor. He has sent me to proclaim release to the captives and recovery of sight to the blind, to let the oppressed go free") provides the foundation for African American sermons on justice and freedom. Failure to use a text as the basis of one's sermon is not preaching. At its best it is storytelling, and at its worst it is a travesty. African American theology of proclamation states that the word preached is not that of the preacher but that of God, who speaks through the preacher. Through the preached word, the justice, mercy, and grace of God are revealed in the congregation of the believers. In most African American denominations the preacher tells of a God who is all-knowing, all-powerful, and present everywhere. Sermons attest to God's being active in the life of the community and residing within the individual through the power of the Holy Spirit. Preaching is kerygmatic, referencing the life, ministry, death, resurrection, and second coming of Jesus. The text is alive and must be associated with the here and now as well as the time of its composition. Exegesis of the text is accomplished through prayers, repeated reading of the text, the preacher's life experiences with the story, and community faith development.

African Americans allow the Bible to speak constructively and critically to each new situation. They strive for political and social justice, confident that the presence of God will bring it to fruition. Use of the Bible solidifies theological grounds for the struggle against injustice. The Bible is established and appropriated on grounds the individual can understand, one's own language, idioms, and needs. The Bible is the chief component of the Black Christian experience and enables cultural and spiritual myths to function in the life of the faith community. Belief in the infallibility of Scripture is based on one's denomination, education, geographical residence, and age.

The exhortation in Black preaching is to inspire, give hope, and declare the eternal watchfulness of a God who never slumbers or sleeps (Isa. 40:28–31). Addressing social and political issues and outlining social ministries are paramount in the preaching event. The preacher through the sermon seeks to preserve the oral tradition, reminds the people of cultural values, instills compassion for all persons, and keeps hope for change burning in the hearts and minds of the community.[4] The task of the preacher is to unearth what is being said about Black women and Black men, particularly in relation to the sexist-racist contradictions of the text. The preacher has an obligation to instruct the listeners in defining, interpreting, and solving contemporary issues of life that overwhelm the people.[5]

Black preaching encompasses classic texts on justice, freedom, and liberation. Men and women have preached these texts to give hope to the congregations and supply possibilities for reconstruction of the world to what God intended it to be. The story of the Exodus out of Egypt is preached as deliverance from all oppression and God's promise to all of God's children for full, plenteous lives. Moses at the Red Sea focuses on leadership when the people want to return to conditions of domination because of fear of the unknown. The imagery used in the Black preaching of Moses standing on the rock and God sending winds to open up the sea and the children of Israel walking across on dry ground has its roots in slavery. The drowning of pharaoh's army paints a picture of removal of one's enemies. Experienced or seasoned preachers and those who imagine the setting are able to place one at the sea and enable one to feel the wind, water, and dirt as one moves from oppression to freedom. The episodes of Daniel in the lions' den and the three Hebrews in the fiery furnace may be preached as hope for God's coming justice or God's rescue of God's children from every kind of distress. In these texts the preacher uses images of politicians, leaders, employers, and even church administrators to depict a God who controls everything. Ezekiel and the valley of dry bones, Elijah on Mount Carmel, and Revelation's "number that no one could number" are staples in the repertoire of Black preachers. The nature and power of the Holy Spirit are necessary for life in community and equality among persons. The stories of Jesus as the Judge, Jury, and Justifier of our lives are essential to Black preaching. The miracles of Jesus involve healing of persons and communities. Some texts are appropriated with a hermeneutic of suspicion (refusal to accept the status quo or traditional understanding and use of the text), ignoring the oppressive nature of the texts or reinterpreting the texts with a cultural hermeneutic. Social justice is the elimination of economic deprivation and social segregation. The preacher takes the words of Holy Scripture and makes new theological formulations that provide hope for those who have not attained justice. One has hope when one hears of the redemptive activity of God in human history through "what God has done, is doing and will do" in the life of the people. The sermon event is to "preach into being" the justice of God.[6]

The Black preacher is to deconstruct life as it exists, undergird the sermon with how God wants life to be, and reconstruct community so that it is able to move to where God wants it to be. Regardless of the texts selected, the focus of the sermon is to be on personal and communal obedience to God. The preacher does not demand perfection or preach easy or cheap grace. The preacher must challenge the listener with examination of self and community and fuller personal engagement of the biblical text. The preacher must relay hope for change from present realities to future possibilities. Finally, the preacher is to lead the community in celebration of what God has done, is doing, and will do in their lives. The preacher seeks to open up means for all of God's children to stand on equal footing. The preacher critiques the inequities in interpersonal relationships, families, communities, churches, and the world.

The irony of Black preaching, yesterday and today, is that the power dynamics of human existence at times lead the newly liberated to mirror the models of their oppressors. In the quest for human and civil rights, at times Black male preachers have stood in the church house rather than the school house or state house door and denied Black female preachers entrance by any means necessary.

The ecclesiastical apartheid evident in twentieth-century churches is part of the assimilation of dominant cultural values that numerous Black denominations have undergone over the past two hundred years. A sort of cultural amnesia has been demonstrated by the men who stood with women for freedom of the race. The Black pulpit became a sanctuary for the perceived power of the Black male to the exclusion of the Black female. Biblical imperatives aside, the social understanding of the place of women in the church and in the world overshadowed the will of God and the "priesthood of all believers." In Africa women were essential to the cultural and religious practices of the community. North American slave narratives spoke of women priests, prophetesses, and queen mothers. Female griots, or storytellers, were the memory banks for the large genealogies of African Americans. Women were the prayer warriors who participated in all forms of worship. They were the link for the ceremonial, ritual, artistic, and social foundations of Black culture.[7]

As early as the nineteenth century, Black women participated in religious and secular assemblies in various capacities. Jarena Lee was the first Black woman to approach a mainline Black denomination for preaching rights.[8] In 1809 she conveyed a request for a license to preach to Rev. Richard Allen, the leader of the oldest Black denomination, the African Methodist Episcopal Church. She was told in that year that the denomination had no law permitting women to preach. In 1817 she was officially given permission to preach but was never ordained. Lee walked more than 2,325 miles in one year, preaching 178 sermons about the just nature of God. She challenged the prejudice of the A.M.E. Church and affirmed the right for women to preach in these excerpts from her 1849 autobiography:

> Oh how careful ought we to be lest through our by-laws of church government and discipline, we bring into disrepute even the word of life. Of as unseemingly as it may appear now-a-days for a woman to preach, it should be remembered that nothing is impossible to God. And why should it be thought impossible, heterodox, or improper for a woman to preach? Seeing that the Saviour died for the woman as well as for the man.

> If the man may preach, because the Saviour died for him, why not the woman? Seeing he died for her also. Is he not a whole Saviour, instead of a half one? As those who hold it wrong for a woman to preach would seem to make it appear.

> Did not Mary *first* preach the risen Saviour, and is not the doctrine of the resurrection the very climax of Christianity—hangs not all our hope on this, as argued by St. Paul? Then did not Mary, a woman, preach the gospel? For she preached the resurrection of the crucified Son of God.[9]

Jarena Lee knew that her call and authority were from God and that she must tell the world about the equality of God. She stated that "God made manifest his power in a manner sufficient to show the world that I was called to labor according to my ability, and the grace given unto me."[10]

Although Black women are central to the development of individual spirituality through teaching or social/political criticism, preaching has remained an almost exclusive male endeavor. African American professor of music and liturgy Melva Costen lists four pillars of worship in African American Christian worship—prayer, song, testimonies, and preaching.[11] All four are inherent in the cultural oral tradition as the people of faith communicate with God. Preaching is traditionally a male event to "break the Bread of Life" or "Tell it" about God's goodness and commands so that all the brothers and (sisters) will be fed.[12] Historically, African American women take leadership in prayer, music, and testimonies. Older women are often called "prayer warriors," citing the concerns of the community and lifting them up fervently to God. Many women use songs as an alternative form of preaching. This allows them an opportunity to speak publicly about biblical texts and their personal experiences and to sing. Often African American women are termed "evangelists" when they demonstrate the gift of song and sacred speech. Familiar lyrics are included in sermons in Black preaching, and gifted preachers sing before or after the sermon. African American women give testimonies or witness the blessings, gifts, and grace of God within the congregational setting, most likely during a Wednesday night prayer meeting or a Sunday morning service. The testimony tells the people of the presence of God in that person's life and is a demonstration of faith. Preachers often refer to a testimony within the context of a sermon. The number of women in preaching ministries, whether in mainline Black religious bodies or nondenominational churches or as independent evangelists, has increased substantially over the past ten years. However, there is much to accomplish in establishing justice and equality within the Black church and for Black women preachers in general.

Black male preachers have used biblical imperatives, made blistering comments about women's sexuality, applied family pressures, dispatched women to outposts of mission, or just plain ignored women's calls as ways of keeping themselves in the male power-laden pulpit. Black male preachers often refer to women in sermons. There are as many who offer exclusively negative examples of women as there are who present positive images and illustrations. The stance depends on the preacher's education, age, geographical area, denominational position on ordination of women, and experiences or relationships with women preachers. Some male preachers deify mothers and wives (e.g., referring to the woman of Prov. 31), yet avoid stories or examples of biblical or contemporary women who were or are leaders, prophets, or disciples. They seem to be caught in the "extraordinary woman" syndrome that mirrors the "good Negro" of the 1950s and 1960s in white male Protestant sermons.

Black women have a task of preaching justice with Black men and women and other groups in order to affirm the rights of all persons. A formidable obstacle I faced in entering ordained ministry was the number of women who spoke out against my call. I am still amazed at the number of women preachers across denominations who rely on decidedly male-oriented language, cite examples of "evil" women, preach human-defined submission rather than biblically sound definitions of submission, and relegate other women to voiceless positions and following the "party" line. Living out the sermonic message or exhibiting a praxis of justice is as vital as preaching about justice, regardless of gender.

WOMANIST BEGINNINGS OF RENOVATION

Using the tools of renovation such as a fresh reading of the text, relentlessly engaging injustice, articulating her standard of justice, and carving out her own space, the African American woman preacher can begin the renovation of "sorrow's kitchen." Renovation is a slow process, but each new sermon is a blueprint for justice. Harlem Renaissance author Zora Neale Hurston depicts the lives of many African American women who have struggled to engage the complexities of their faith and injustices in the world.[13] This struggle usually is waged in systems within a relatively oppressive and exclusive societal atmosphere. Sorrow's kitchen is that place where African American women are told who they are, what they can do, and how they are to act. It is often within the walls of churches, which are described as bastions of God's love and Christ's liberation and equality, that Black women are labeled as evil and valueless. They are responsible for the downfall of Black men, are poor mothers whose children are part of a lost generation, and are ignorant pawns of the larger society. It is the place where women's faith is relegated to the back pews, under lace caps and white gloves, to indicate their submission to male authority. Sorrow's kitchen is the place where voices are silenced, thoughts are monitored, and sacrifice is demanded. It is the room within God's house reserved for women only.

In their search for justice—the basic right of all persons to God's benefits and resources—African American women have "licked out all the pots." They have encountered racism, sexism, classism, materialism, denominationalism, ageism, and other forms of oppression and rejection. They have attempted to find their own voices. Many strive to chart their own paths to live out their faith in God. They have stood boldly, inside and outside the Black church, against an array of charges that they are "going against God's Word" or that they are "trying to be men" by preaching the gospel or acknowledging their calls to ministry. They have been socially ostracized, they have been expelled from churches, and they have experienced abuse and control of their minds and bodies by power structures said to represent God.

African American women preachers also hold the Bible as central to the preaching event. Although the Bible is often used to marginalize Black women, they continue to use it by "widening the margins" of the text. Katie Cannon says that African American women open the Bible wide enough to see themselves within the text.[14] They seek egalitarian, inclusive readings of the text. Black women must be aware of the submerged issues and expressions in the texts as well as those operating in the larger society. In the Black community biblical literalism has been used to deny women ordination. The womanist hermeneutic is that any denial of dignity or equality particularly based on biblical usage is a sin. Cannon remarks that Black preaching is to "make it plain" so that stories of faith passed down intergenerationally come to life. African American women preachers, depending on denomination, education, and ordination status, seek to balance the spoken word with the political aims of the sermon. Womanist hermeneutics seek to contemporize Scripture in an emancipatory process that speaks to the entire faith community. The womanist preacher must "slough off" subversive memories while proclaiming the religious inheritance of "ancestral mothers and fathers that enhances narrative variation for audience responses in similar but new situations."[15]

Religious historian Judith Weisenfeld writes about the importance of Black women's stories in faith development:

> Religious experience as a grounding for African American women's sense of self and ability to participate in the formulation of communal identities stands as a significant thread connecting the individual stories of African American women. Through intimate spiritual experiences, African American women's stories often emphasize they gained the assurance of divine guidance and, as a result, found the power to speak, to organize, to lead and to hope for all things possible.[16]

African American women choose passages that speak to their existential dilemma. Due to the number of times women are assigned or invited to speak at Women's Day services or women's conferences, there is an abundance of attention to the stories of women, named and unnamed in the Bible. One of the biblical women cited in preaching by African American women is Hagar. There is a strong identification with her role as surrogate, her treatment by Sarah, the use and misuse by Abraham, and the expulsion with her son into the desert. Hagar mirrors the lives of slave mothers and the stereotypical treatment of many contemporary African American women. Recurrent references to Deborah, Mary Magdalene, Tamar, Jephthah's daughter, Vashti, the woman at the well, the woman bent over, the woman with the issue of blood, Tabitha, the Candace, Ruth, and the Queen of Sheba appear in sermons by Black women. The circumstances of the lives of these women speak of God's "leveling the ground at the foot of the cross"—God's salvific action in the lives of faithful women. There is a hope that "what God does for others God will do for you." African American women also use the cultural classic texts that seek to demonstrate God's just nature for all persons, not just Black women. African American women preachers, depending on denomination and expectations, share a common theme of equality and liberation in their sermon composition. They also preach topical sermons on justice, love, community, liberation, and responsibility.

The Bible is a self-corrective to a range of attitudes about justice. There may be a preoccupation with theodicy—how to account for the justice of God in light of the persistence of suffering and inequality. Through Bible studies, sermons, songs, liturgies, prayers, and daily experience, Black women engage the biblical texts and determine for themselves the interpretation that affirms their humanity. They identify their own experience in the Bible as an existential reality.

Old Testament professor Renita Weems postulates that African American women continue to respond to the Bible as meaningful despite its oppressive use.[17] Interpretation depends on social location of the preacher and her particular hermeneutic, imagination, and creativity. Marginalized readers have the task and responsibility of restoring oppressed voices, breaking the chains from the texts, and opening them up to all persons. Black women select preaching passages yielding hope of a liberated world. Reems describes the richness of those passages: "The oppressed are liberated, the last become first, the humbled are exalted, the despised are preferred, those rejected are welcomed, the long-suffering are rewarded, the dispossessed are repossessed, and the arrogant are prostrated. And these are the passages for the oppressed readers, that stand at the center of the biblical message and thereby, serve as a vital form of biblical faith."[18]

Through total engagement with the text, reading it through the eyes and lives of Black women, the African American female preacher establishes her own hermeneutic and liberation motif. Educator Anna Julia Cooper wrote in 1892, "Only the Black woman can say when and where I enter."[19]

She alone can know the depths of despair and societal subjugation experienced by Black women. The issues of inequality faced by African American women emanate not only from the Black church and community but also from the larger society. Recognizing the subjugation of Black women because of race, gender, class, and even body type exacerbates their struggle for justice. In addition, some Black women preachers continue the legacy of oppressive sermons by modeling language, imagery, and metaphors used by Black men and other preachers who routinely relegate Black women to sorrow's kitchen.

As Black women find their fuller voices in preaching, they can then say when and where they will be free. Making certain choices for sermonic material, responsibly using the biblical text, defining themselves as preachers, and preaching on despite the obstacles are essential to the furtherance of African American women preaching about justice. Black women have their own ideas about justice and seek an opportunity to dialogue with the church and community. If one avenue is closed, such as pulpit ministry, Black women have opened other highways for self-expressions—music, poetry, teaching, cooking, and/or quilting. Still, in the Black church context the preaching event has the highest value. Until there is a critical mass of women preaching and men and women willing to support Black women preachers, preaching justice in the pulpit and in the pews will be tentative. Justice in the community will be in flux. It is easier for society to accept an African American woman teaching or leading a company than leading and preaching at a church, regardless of location, denomination, or skills.

Despite the negative implications of the status of African American women preachers, we continue to preach. Our presence in the pulpit alone is a visual for justice. Each time one of us preaches or reads Scripture someone has a new image of preachers, the preaching moment, and a just society. The cultural saying "It's another star in the crown" or "It's another brick in my brand-new home" means that each small step gets us closer to the mark. Life teaches us lessons that we naturally use during the preaching moment. Whether the road had been rough or smooth, the context of our lives provides substance for sermon imagery. If we preach only about how hard becoming a preacher has been based on gender, we have given over to the forces seeking to keep women out of pulpits. The blame game works only a limited time, then people stop listening. If we place at the center of preaching both the obstructions to justice and the biblical imperatives for equality, most can begin to visualize possibilities for transformation. Justice is attainable. In essence if we tear down strongholds, we must provide alternative shelters for all of the people—female and male, oppressors and oppressed, good and bad, and so on. The next step is to jointly construct new buildings within which everyone may work, dwell, and contribute based on gifts and not political machinations.

Having grown up in the Black church, I recognize that with all of its problems it is still the "fertile crescent" of my preaching. The Black church allows me to paint pictures with color, sound, and body language. It allows me to experience freedom and a sense of equality for those few hours and to gain a sense of what it means to be accepted as a useful, whole person. Images I have written down during sermon preparation are often guided by an awareness of the persons for whom I am preaching. Metaphors and images I have found helpful in composing sermons have been taken from life experiences, encounters with a variety of cultures, diverse faith systems, newspapers, television, and occupations. The most important source for images and metaphors in the preaching event has been the indwelling of the Holy Spirit, which connects me with the people, their needs, the unity of belief, common distresses, and shared victories. This sharing as community, knowing the stories of the faith and the history of my people, and honoring my unique position as a woman who preaches strengthen my resolve to seek and preach justice not only within the Black church but also within the church universal.

Borrowing from culture, I have used images of the mothers who always have room for one more, who can take one chicken and feed twenty people. This image parallels God's abundance as well as the practice of hospitality. Being turned down for loans or denied credit for housing but still finding the means to obtain food, clothing, and shelter is used in conjunction with the Elijah story about the widow whose mill and oil were constantly replenished. Children in day care or elementary school who play together sometimes disagree, yet can sit next to each other without prejudice. Having worked with persons with disabilities for many years as a speech-language pathologist, I remember that during the Special Olympics if one person fell down, all the other young people would go back and help that person up, then they would all cross the line together. This is the beloved community, not the power-hungry world we have come to know. After living in Denver for fifteen years, I could look at the mountains and begin to see that the climb to freedom, justice, and equality is not straight up the side of the hill. The path to the top of the mountain is winding, with hairpin turns, and every now and then it looks as if one will fall off the side into a pit, a lake, or trees. One must stop and gather strength, but the ascent is worth it. The struggle for justice is costly, freighted with danger, but one must risk death to reach the summit.

I found my voice because the pressure on my vocal folds was too much. African American women's issues and striving for justice are particular in nature but shared by all. Achieving and maintaining justice, with everyone sharing in the communion and each person coming with the same invitation, can be accomplished only if all have a say in what justice is and how it may be realized. Each of us, ordained or nonordained, preaches by what we say as much as where and how we say it.

"DIFFERENT KITCHENS WITH MOUNTAIN VIEWS"

African American women have been preaching justice for centuries. They have preached on street corners, in prisons, by sickbeds, in schools, in small groups, in women's Bible studies, in choirs, in prayer meetings, in churches, in homes, and any place they could say a word for God. Many remain in traditional Black denominations, which may or may not ordain them. Some opt for nondenominational settings or start their own churches. A large number become evangelists, traveling the country like the preachers of the nineteenth century, such as Jarena Lee and Sojourner Truth. Still others teach, sing, and testify about God's goodness in more socially acceptable alternatives to preaching. Others leave the church altogether, broken and battered from the weight of oppression. There is, of course, injustice in the larger society for women in general and for African American women in particular based on age-old stereotypes and social restrictions. Yet there are women who unashamedly lift up the name of Jesus in the congregation of the saints, whether there are two or two thousand listeners. The very act of calling oneself a preacher moves an African American woman from sorrow's kitchen to the peaky mountain, at least for a short time. The renovation will open up the way for more women to talk about a just society and begin to live spiritually and physically within one. As long as African American women are preaching justice, people will hear, and eventually, people will act and join their voices to the chorus of "Freedom Now!"

The following two sermon fragments focus on justice for all persons. Written from a womanist perspective, they have been preached in their entirety for special Women's Day programs, regular Sunday morning services, and national conferences. Their purpose is decidedly to renovate sorrow's kitchen and move all the hearers, including the preacher, to the peaky mountain.

Are We Doing Justice or Just Us?

> And what does [God] require of you?
> To act justly and to love mercy
>   and to walk humbly with your God. (Mic. 6:8 NIV)

> The Spirit of [God] is on me
>   because he has anointed me
>   to preach good news to the poor.
> He has sent me to proclaim freedom for the prisoners
>   and recovery of sight for the blind,
> to release the oppressed. (Luke 4:18 NIV)

Fraud. Bribery. Gangs. Corruption. Violence. Bigotry. Insensitivity. Murder. Children killing parents. Parents abusing children. Public officials oppressing the poor. New laws to control how people live and who is fit to die. Sound familiar? This is 1997, but the same thing was reported in the *Judah Daily News* in 742 B.C.E. Walk back through the sacred text with me to the time of the southern working-class prophet Micah. This contemporary of Isaiah and Hosea was assigned by God to tell the people that their lives were offensive to God. Micah was called to plead the case of the people before God. The mountains testified about the high places people had built, altars to other gods like power, prestige, money, etc. Micah begins to give Judah, the defendant, a verdict from God in a three-point sermon that still applies to believers today.

Micah tells us that as a covenant people, in agreement, in contract with God, we are each charged to remember our blessings and benefits and to extend them to others. God's justice is our standard. Justice is not about *just us* but is the delivery of God's mercy, love, and grace to all creation. Justice is honesty, impartiality, fairness for all of God's people. Whatever God does is just even if the result is not by our standards.

Micah 6:8: "And what does [God] require of us but to *do* justice?" Not to talk but to act. Not to theorize but to practice justice. We are called to defend the poor and powerless, end victimization, and break down barriers and prejudice. God wants justice. It is not a request; it is a requirement of our contract, our testament, our covenant with God. Justice implies action, dynamic acts. It is the act of providing a space for equal access to God. Injustice is stagnant, corroded, immobile faith. Justice means we get up off our stools of discontent, grumbling, complaints, and finger-pointing; move out into the world; and struggle for the cause of freedom. Justice obliterates we-they, those people, you people, those Baptists, those Black people, you women, those homeless, and anyone who doesn't walk like, talk like, smell like, look like, think like, and act like we do.

I hear Amos say, "But let justice roll down like waters, and righteousness like an everflowing stream." Justice is not measured in teaspoons, legislated to conserve the rights of any particular group, or doled out by the vote of a few good men and sometimes women. Justice sweeps, surges, moves, clearing out, cleaning up whatever is not of God. We need to rejoice in the fact that God does not always give us what we deserve but supplies all our needs.

My brothers and my sisters, we do not have permission to be selective in our compassion. We cannot do checkbook ministry. We must be personally involved in the lives of others. The role of the church is to meet people where they are, help them when we can, and let God use them as God sees fit. Jesus came to us with a ministry of care and compassion. Can we do any less? Are we doing justice to the poor, blind, locked out, locked down, dispossessed, deferred, depressed? Are we ministering to all of God's people or just our family, our friends, our church, our race, our school, ourselves? Are we doing justice as God intended, or are we doing just us? Have we elected ourselves judge and jury, determining who is worthy, or do we remember that only God is worthy? Have we joined the conspiracy of silence that allows injustice to rule, or do we ask God to strengthen our resolve, put steel in our social backbone, and stand up for freedom regardless of what it costs? Will we protect all the children? Will we stop looking the other way when someone is in danger?

In the earthquaking of our lives, the love of God covers us. In the flood plains of indecision, the power of the Spirit lifts us to dry ground. In the catastrophic places of our neighborhoods today and tomorrow, God never fails to send the rain of renewal and the hedge of protection. God has done so much for us, and the *hesed* of God continues to give us access to God's blessing. What are we doing in return? Are we doing justice or just us?

GOD'S AFFIRMATIVE ACTION PROGRAM

A voice cries out:
"In the wilderness prepare the way of [God],
    make straight in the desert a highway for our God.
Every valley shall be lifted up,
    and every mountain and hill be made low;
the uneven ground shall become level,
    and the rough places a plain.

Then the glory of [God] shall be revealed,
　　and all people shall see it together,
　　　for the mouth of [God] has spoken." (Isa. 40:3–5)

And just then there appeared a woman with a spirit that had crippled her for eighteen years. She was bent over and was quite unable to stand up straight. When Jesus saw her, he called her over and said, "Woman, you are set free from your ailment." When he laid his hands on her, immediately she stood up and began praising God. (Luke 13:11–13)

Our lives are permeated with opposites, power dynamic, ways of seeing one another that at times keep us from being freely who and what God wants us to be. We have all heard of the Affirmative Action Program, the controversial government program that was supposed to level the playing ground for all persons in terms of employment, education, and housing. This program was to end discrimination, equalize debts, and make society one in which all persons had equal access to the benefits of freedom. Somehow in our humanity, especially in our church community, we seem to have it all wrong. We are going backward. We have allowed laws, polity, power trips to overshadow God's Affirmative Action Program. You know the one that says we are all God's children, that the Spirit was sent to everyone who received it, that there is plenty good room in God's kingdom. My sisters and my brothers, there is nothing new under the sun. God is not pleased with how we treat one another, but God has a program that will make it all brand-new.

One Sabbath Jesus was teaching on perseverance, repentance, and eternal life in synagogue. He was surrounded by men, and according to the law of the day, the women were in the courtyard in back listening. The Bible says that Jesus stopped his message because he saw a woman. Not just a woman in the minds of other women but a woman who according to law wasn't even supposed to be in the synagogue. This woman had a "spirit of infirmity." She had been physically and mentally bent over for eighteen years. It doesn't say she was born bent over; it says she had an infirmity. No name, no nationality, no information on her people or where she lived. She was bent over. She couldn't straighten up. Her face saw only the dirt. The pressure on her spine must have been tremendous, as if she was carrying the weight of the world on her shoulders.

I imagine she knew the law, but she had heard about Jesus and something within her told her on this day to find him for herself. On this day

Jesus saw her through the needs of others. Jesus looked at her and said, "Today, not tomorrow, not when the laws change, not when there is a critical mass, not when all the men are dead, not when the melting pot no longer simmers, but this day you are free." On this day Jesus took her diminished status as a woman, against the laws of the land, and spoke to her. Jesus called upon her faith. Jesus touched her. Jesus prayed for her. Jesus assured her of her forgiveness. Jesus commanded a change in her life. Jesus defended her healing before the leaders of the church.

The miracle was not over. This woman had not had the energy for eighteen years to speak for herself. The Book says that she stood up praising God. The weight of oppression on our hearts and minds at times keeps us from praising God. The pressure to be someone or something we are not freezes our vocal folds. We become like rabbits with no voice, just following the command of others. The overwhelming sense of inadequacy becomes self-destructive. But know that on this day Jesus speaks to our hearts and says, "You are free." This same Jesus sees each of us as a person created in the image of God. Jesus sees us as free, not bent over with the pressures and restrictions of life. We are all equal in God's sight, not inferior or superior. Today, you are free of whatever is keeping you down. You are free of those who said you wouldn't make it or amount to anything of value.

God's grace allows us to reveal our full selves, to stretch beyond any social barrier. God is able to heal our souls, minds, and bodies. God accepts us as we are and cleans us up to be instruments of peace. God is present in our lives even when we feel bent over. Know that during our process of being elevated, God is about the business of empowering us and restoring our hope. In God's Affirmative Action Program all things are possible. In God's Affirmative Action Program the whole person is considered, regardless of social status, age, race, rank, or gender. In God's Affirmative Action Program nothing and nobody can keep us from God's love and mercy. I hear God saying to us today, "You may feel bent over but you are not broken." Just like the woman bent over, we need to move out of the box some people have us in and move into new spiritual homes where we can see Jesus for ourselves. We need to go deep inside ourselves to that place the Spirit resides and "have a little talk with Jesus." Listen for the voice of Jesus, saying, "Come unto me *all* you that labor and are heavy laden and *I will* give you rest." I'm a witness that God will send you back bent no more and praising God's name.

CHAPTER FOUR

A Filipino Perspective

"Unfinished Dream" in the Land of Promise

Eleazar S. Fernandez

To know the plight of a people, it takes more than a tourist acquaintance with their experience; even much more is needed to articulate their deepest pain as well as soaring hope. For a few years now I have had this privilege of a beyond-tourist experience since I moved into the land of the free and home of the brave—the United States of America—and journeyed with Asian Americans in their pain, joy, and hope. It is out of this experience that I venture to write this chapter on preaching.

Theology and the Ministry of Preaching

Preaching, even as it is an activity shared by all preachers, is not always understood theologically in a similar way. Given this situation, I see the need to explicitly state my theological premises on preaching. This, in my view, is best understood by dealing with the theological presuppositions of preaching in relation to the overall ministry of the church.

Preaching as Theological Act: Preachers as Theologians

I could not agree more when preachers say that preaching is first and foremost a "theological act."[1] It is an act because it proclaims a theological event and participates in that event; it does not only have a "theological context but is itself a theological act."[2] Whatever else is involved in preaching, it is primarily a proclamation of the Word of God. The preacher makes use of various tools of communication and engages in analysis (textual and social), but the direction is theological discernment, articulation, and proclamation. Giving primacy to the theological act should not be overlooked if the integrity of preaching—and other disciplines—is to be maintained.

There is always the temptation to forget that preaching is first and foremost a theological act, perhaps more so among persons who are strongly committed to preach the gospel as it relates to social issues. Thus, the reminder that preaching is a theological act is relevant and urgent. Yet even when preachers are in concert in saying that preaching is a theological act, the theological undergirding of this claim is construed in various, and sometimes conflicting, ways. It is even fairly common to find, as in my encounter among pastors and church members in the denomination where I belong (United Church of Christ in the Philippines), those who equate the "theological" with the "biblical," and the "biblical" with narrow "biblicism." When this happens, everything else becomes distorted: there is no critical reading of the classical texts and no appropriate analysis of the social world of the community of believers. Because preaching, in the context of my years in the pastoral ministry and involvement in the training of pastors (Theological Education by Extension or TEE), suffered from these major distortions, I did not only have to engage in conscientization work, but I also had to teach about methods of interpreting texts. (Conscientization is a term used by Latin American liberation theologians to refer to the process of coming to a critical social and political consciousness.)

If preaching is primarily a theological act, what is the theological thrust of this act? For me the general thrust of Christian preaching is the proclamation of God's liberating, saving, and reconciling love as witnessed in the life and ministry of Jesus and the "Christic" community that revolved around him. It involves a prophetic naming of destructive forces and the proclamation of a profoundly new sensibility and ethics. It may also involve giving comfort to afflicted persons, enabling communities to survive and thrive, and offering hope in the midst of hopelessness, but it is never a therapy for psychic numbing or utopian escape or poetic abandonment of the present. Instead, full generosity is given to the present in light of the promised future, and the present is not sacrificed for the sake of the future.

Although preaching the gospel has a general thrust, it needs to address the concrete situations of people, for the gospel is no gospel at all unless it becomes specific. The gospel that is not specific or concrete may even be counter to the gospel. When confronted with diversity, it is a common pulpit discourse in the United States to project a universal (e.g., equality in the sight of God), which is most often a particular dominant perspective masquerading as universal. This kind of discourse is "assimilationist" and "melting pot" in its intent and consequences.

An Asian Indian way of thinking, on the other hand, provides an approach that is useful for preachers. Diversity is not reduced to a common denominator or to a universal abstraction. It may help to illustrate this point by asking, What is common among rivers? The usual answer is "riverness," for it is the common denominator of all rivers. Instead of talking about "riverness" (common denominator), an approach abstracting the common among rivers, in the Asian Indian approach the common to all rivers is the ocean. The universal (common) does not impoverish the particular; rather, the universal (common) becomes the fullness and enrichment of the particular.[3] To put it in another way, instead of talking in singular about "ability to love," the preacher talks about "abilities to love" or about "ways to love." God's love is not a monotonous uniformity, but has multiple expressions in response to the plight of a people, and this, for Asian Americans, is shaped by their experience.

Preaching and theology exist in a relationship of mutuality, an idea I share with other preachers.[4] Theology, with its metaphoric or "is" and "is not" character, enables us to see through the pathos of the people not only the "what is" but also the "what might be" or the dreamed-for future. This demands that "one must learn not only to think and read poetically but also must build and dwell poetically."[5] The "what is" and the "what might be" as well as the "thinking and building poetically" in theology find articulation and proclamation in the preaching event.

Among Korean Americans the concept of *han* (deep anguish and pain due to experience of oppression) stands at the intersection of the "what is" and the "what might be"; it points to both the painful reality and the poetic longing for what is yet to come. It is the duty of Asian American preachers to lift up the *han* of the people and proclaim God's prophetic no along with the gospel of hope and healing. Preachers must give voice to this *han* in the context of worship. An Asian liturgy of worship expresses this deep *han* that women experience:

Loving God . . .
We know that in many of our sisters and brothers
Your image has been scarred and tarnished,
They have been drained by exploitation;
Your image has been destroyed
By people subjugating one another;

The female part of your image
Has been conveniently forgotten;
But you meant your creation to be good,
Your image to be whole.[6]

THE CONTEXT OF PREACHING
AND TOOLS OF SOCIOLOGICAL MEDIATION

Preaching, which is indeed a theological act, does not float in some kind of theological limbo. It arises out of a context and it goes back to a context. Preachers often speak of addressing the context, but in reality they understand and give value to the context in conflicting ways. Because preaching is primarily a theological act, even the consideration of context is theological.[7]

Many preachers treat the world (context) as a backdrop or a stage in God's mighty act of saving human beings. This treatment of the world, having no theological value except as a stage of God's mighty acts, also warrants the hermeneutical treatment of the world as *passive* receiver or receptacle vis-à-vis the *active* eternal Word of God. There is more theologically, however, to a context than a medium, space, or receptacle for the message to become intelligible. Society or the social dimension must come into the direct purview of preaching not simply because it is a backdrop or the stage in which human beings are located, but because the world (cosmos) is embraced by God and because the reality of human beings—their plight and destiny—cannot be treated as if it were separate from the world.

Only in a context (not in a vacuum) does a message become a message or a revelation become a revelation. I do not agree that "context is just a receptacle of revelation," which is the theological undergirding of some preachers who talk about context. Instead, following Asian theologian C. S. Song, "context and revelation are united to tell the world what truth is." More appropriately, "there is no such thing as *mere* context," but "revelation *became* context" or "revelation *is* in context."[8] This means that Asian American Christians need not be culturally whitewashed in order to hear the gospel, and that their very own sociocultural context can become an avenue of God's revelation.

What does the unity of context and revelation mean for interpreting biblical texts and for preaching? The Pentecost account (Acts 2:1–13) would elucidate my point and would provide an idea on how to preach it from a different perspective. I concur with Andrew Sung Park, a Korean American theologian, in his observation that the Pentecost account is often, if not always, interpreted as primarily a propagation of the universal gospel. The mere fact that they were talking different languages does not count for anything at all. Instead of simply construing the speaking in tongues as a vehicle for the transmittal of the gospel, Park argues that "we need . . . to see that the event itself [speaking in various tongues] was the very content of the gospel, not its mere form."[9] Asian American preachers must craft a sermon that conveys to the people that speaking in their own tongues is good news, being able to express one's deepest feelings in a language close to one's heart is good news; and having various languages and cultures in the United States is not bad news but good news.

Context is not a mere container of God's revelation. My use of socioanalytic tools in preaching flows from this theological premise. I do not use the socioanalytic tools in preaching as mere instruments to dissect a passive context. The analytic tools themselves, which may come in the form of stories, parables, and narratives, are part and parcel of the revelatory event. A parable of a sick person in Asia, which I heard and have used in my sermons (the source of which I cannot establish), weaves for us the need to consider the world seriously in its complexity and the use of social analysis, the theological discernment, and the call to action. The parable runs this way:

> Once upon a time there was a person in Asia who was afflicted with a terrible ailment. Four of his friends came to visit him and offered their help. The first came and said: "You must have a headache. Your body is hot. Here, take some aspirin and antibiotic to relieve your pain."
>
> The second friend came and sadness dawned on his face. He felt great pity for his sick friend and with words of compassion said: "My heart cries for you, my friend."
>
> Then the third friend came, looked at the sick person, and raised his moral complaint to God: "Why, God, when others are healthy and happy, do you let my friend suffer from a terrible pain? This is unfair and unjust!"
>
> Finally, the fourth friend came for a visit and was terribly saddened by the plight of his sick friend. Sensing that his friend was in deep agony, he said: "You have been suffering from your headache for several days now. I think you must see a doctor and get a thorough checkup. There is a medical clinic in the next town; I can take you there." So they went to the clinic and had the sick person undergo a series of tests, X rays, and analyses. It was discovered that the person had a tumor. The fourth friend

explored several resources available and asked the help of others. He took care of his friend until he regained his health.

Now, which of these four friends was the real friend to the sick person? Which of these friends truly responded to the plight of the sick friend?

This parable conveys the need to examine seriously the context in which the sermon is delivered. Through the form of a parable, the preacher can lead the people in the stages of analysis until they see the systemic ailment. Of course, the sermon must be in sync with the overall ministry of the church. It is important that the preacher does not run too fast and leave the congregation behind. Preachers do not come from the outside pulling the people into the promised future, but they are companions in the journey. What I say of the theologian in relation to the community is also true of the preacher in relation to the faith community. Preachers are like waves of the ocean. They "happen to be more conspicuous parts of the ocean but themselves are part of the ocean, and of the same substance with it. The ocean will bring forth its waves as the people its [preachers]."[10]

SOCIAL LOCATION, THE PREACHER, AND THE MESSAGE

I grew up in a family in which education is highly valued, especially as a means to get out of poverty and marginalization. I must work hard, my parents constantly admonished me, if I was not to be like our poor neighbors. When I was in college, my parents instructed me not to get involved in politics of radical social transformation, for that would only divert me from the goal of getting out of our sorry situation. But their worst fears came to reality. I became aware of the politics of domination and the suffering of the Filipino people that got me involved in politics of social transformation. As it turned out, my quest for education, which was primarily to escape poverty and suffering, has brought me back into the pains of our world. This experience resonates with the words of Ecclesiastes 1:18: "For in much wisdom is much vexation, and those who increase knowledge increase sorrow." Many times in my life I wish I had not known what I knew, but it torments my soul to pretend as if I had not known.

This experience and awareness of the pains of this world are formative of the way I understand my vocation as a pastor, professor, and preacher. My experience shapes where I locate socially, what I see, and what I preach. As a pastor in some rural areas in the Philippines, I sometimes found myself preaching at a funeral service of a child whose poor parents could not afford to buy a modest coffin that would, at least, prevent the smell of the decaying body from coming out, and the neighborhood seemed to care less in giving a dime to them who needed the most. But when monied parishioners died, more funds went into the coffers of the family of the deceased. Isn't this life cruel and unjust? At that sight, feeling disheartened, I extemporaneously delivered the message that needed to be proclaimed. Confronted with more urgent literal life-and-death concerns of people around me, I was not content dealing with the abstract Trinity, but I preached the gospel in response to the conspiracy of another (unholy) trinity: the absence of breakfast, lunch, and dinner.

In pursuit of further studies and later on a job offer in the United States, I found myself living in another country. My new geographical location confronted me with a new set of concerns, though related to my struggle in the Philippines. In the Philippines the "ism" that preoccupied my attention was classism, but my move to the United States has put racism at the forefront, though the two cannot be separated (along with other forms of "isms": sexism, heterosexism, speciesism, ableism, to name a few). At least, when it comes to class, I could hide myself in my professorial job. But I could not hide my brown skin, my slant eyes, and, of course, my Filipino accent. Every time I go out of the house into the wider white world my skin color influences how I am perceived and received by people. My journey with Asian Americans has led me to experience another form of marginalization (racism), and with it new challenges and new forms of proclaiming the good news.

Surviving and thriving in the situation of multiple marginalization are not easy, but one need not assume a victim mentality in relation to it. There is no inherent goodness in being marginalized, but one can convert the situation into a fertile ground for creative thinking and a jumping point for transformative action. What appears to be a forsaken and barren desert of multiple marginalization can become a dwelling place of the creative spirit. As one who has experienced dislocation and multiple marginalization, I have known what it means to live in multiple worlds: the world where I came from, the world of Asian American life, and the wider world of North American life. And this privilege of having to live in different worlds has taught me that we can live differently as well as imagine and reconstruct a world in which difference is not treated with indifference. It has taught me that we can live in one world/many worlds.[11] The preaching event is, for me, a moment to exhort and to affirm the community that, indeed, we can live differently while we have life and live with integrity according to the demands of the gospel.

Asian American preachers must choose, and many have decided to do so, marginalization as a site of resistance and transformation. I say "must choose," because there is strong pressure both from the congregation and from the wider society for Asian American preachers not to touch issues that rock the boat. Actually, in numerous quarters of Asian American churches and in the wider Asian American populace there is this discouragement of prophetic critique, for doing so is construed as being ungrateful to the benefits that Uncle Sam has bestowed. Thus, Asian American preachers have a task not only of linking the community's faith to the wider society's challenges, but also of raising the prophetic consciousness of their congregations.

DISCERNING THE PLIGHT OF ASIAN AMERICANS

Many Asian Americans have "made it in America," but there are also those who have not, and their stories are often swept under the rug by the whole society and even by their own ethnic groups.

I believe that these submerged stories must be told along with the stories of triumph. Even when my throbbing heart seems to impede the flow of words, I have to articulate the pain of Asian Americans, for I believe that without the words to name this pain, a people is also without words to articulate its profound joy and soaring hope.

AN UPROOTED PEOPLE: EXILES AND STRANGERS FROM FOREIGN SHORES

Pushed by various factors (economic, political, and cultural) in their home-lands, the children of Asia have been pulled to the shores of America. Early on, Asian Americans came to America as part of the labor force to advance the "progress of civilization" in this continent.[12] Leaving their homelands and closely knit communal ties has not been easy for first-generation Asian American immigrants. Many of them would not have considered leaving their countries if the factors (economic, political, cultural) that pushed them were not strong, the most crucial of which was and still is economic marginalization of their homelands within the global capitalist economy. Not even the passage of time could easily erase the strong memories and ties they have from their homelands. For sure, some have made their tran-sition into their new adopted land more quickly than others. Second-generation Asian Americans may readily dismiss this nostalgia, but the strong memories of the first generation cannot be taken lightly, for the mark of uprootedness—of living in two different and often conflicting worlds—is deep. Without strong support from families and friends, many immigrants have suffered from depression and other mental ailments.[13] "I know deep down in my heart," Carlos Bulosan wrote to a friend, "that I am an exile in America."[14]

This exilic experience, especially for first-generation Asian Americans, is so painfully real that Asian American preachers must utter meaningful words to address this plight. A God who journeys or who migrates with them, when uttered by the preacher in an act of worship, is a gospel. Asian Americans can sing God's song in the new land because God is with them: God is not left behind in the Philippines, Thailand, China, Korea, or Japan.

OUTSIDERS-INSIDERS OF THE AMERICAN DREAM

Another wound that compounds the pain of uprootedness of Asian Americans is their experience of being considered outsiders by the dominant group in their adopted homeland. They came to America inflated with hopes of participating in the American Dream. Some did "make it in America," but they soon learned with a shock of recognition the other face of America: America considers them strangers from a foreign shore. *Isang magandang señora, libot na libot ng espada* (There is a beautiful lady surrounded with swords), says the Philippine riddle.[15] Pushed from their homelands by hardships and pulled to America in search of a greener pasture or safety, Asian Americans soon found the land encircled by sharp blades of hostility.

Asian American labor helped build America, yet ironically, white workers have considered Asian American labor a threat, especially when the whites experienced economic misfortunes. But the Asian Americans persisted, survived, and thrived. A high percentage of Asians have been successful in their various fields of endeavors. For this reason and others—working long hours, sometimes more than one job, and not raising complaints—they have earned the title of "model minority."[16] However, Asian Americans take with much caution the designation "model minority." Aside from the fact that this does not take into consideration the plight of those who are at the bottom of the economic scale and the factors that made some Asians "successful," beneath the surface of praise lies the feeling of envy. Invidious comparison between Asian Americans and other ethnic groups has only resulted in increasing hostilities against this "model minority."

Given this particular plight, Asian American preachers are challenged to preach a two-pronged message: first, the gospel's resounding no to discriminatory practices and attempts to scapegoat racial minorities along with the affirmation of the right of all to participate in the American Dream; second, a prophetic critique of the American Dream itself and Asian Americans' participation in the pursuit of "success" in relation to or at the expense of other racial minorities. It is an idolatrous success when, as pointed out by Andrew Sung Park, many Korean businesses "succeed" out of the cheap labor of newly arrived Korean immigrants and other racial minorities.[17]

TRYING HARD TO BE AN AMERICAN: POLITICS OF IDENTITY

"I have been four years in America," a Filipino immigrant in California said sadly, "and I am a stranger. It is not because I want to be. I have tried to be as 'American' as possible. I live like an American, eat like American, and dress the same, and yet everywhere I find Americans who remind me of the fact that I am a stranger."[18]

Not even the children and grandchildren of Asian Americans have found full acceptance as Americans in white America. For the white Americans, Asian Americans are always *Asian* Americans, whereas the whites are simply Americans. When a second-generation Filipino American boy was asked by a white boy where he came from, he simply said, "Minnesota." His response put him into trouble. The white boy forcefully insisted: "*Where are you really from?*" Confronted by this situation, many young Asian Americans have learned to answer the question by stating their parents' country of origin, which does not accurately say who they are. But this, too, invites trouble, for whites often interpret this as a stubborn refusal of Asian Americans to be fully American. And when an Asian American says that he or she belongs to the Third World in the heart of America, more trouble is coming. The most likely verbal attack is: "If you don't like it here why don't you go back to where you came from!"[19]

Responding to the issue of identity is important for Asian American preachers. Asian Americans are *neither* Asian *nor* Americans. This neither-nor status is a source of pain, and Asian American preachers must articulate this pain in their sermons. Though there is nothing good in this pain as such, the preachers must do something to transform this pain into an occasion for prophetic consciousness. There is, however, such an emphasis on the neither-nor or being in the "in-between" that the positive aspect, which is the "in-both" (Asians *and* Americans), is often neglected. I am calling to task Asian American preachers to articulate Asian Americans' "in-both" identity.

RELATIONSHIP OF SUBORDINATION AND ABUSE

Aside from getting a higher education, marrying an American is, for many Asians, a passport to a better life. Men and women, but mostly women, seek relationships with Americans, regardless of personal character and physical appearance, for the sole purpose of coming to the United States. Various means are usually employed to establish the relationship. An overstaying Filipina tourist who worked illegally—a former teacher, married and with children—was forced to marry in order to change her visa status. She even paid the man with her hard-earned money to become her husband. It turned out that the man was sexually and physically abusive, and he constantly harassed her for more money with the threat of reporting her to the immigration officials.[20] Hers is not an isolated phenomenon. I have come to know some people in similar situations. They endure the abusive relationship and do not report to the proper authorities for fear that their bid for a green card or U.S. citizenship may be jeopardized.

There are, of course, persons who are legally and happily married to U.S. citizens, and as I mentioned earlier, they are generally women. One can easily perceive a relationship of equality when both spouses are highly educated. But in a case of a mail-order bride, where the bride is most often of lower academic and professional status, a relationship of subordination is prevalent. I know of some cases where wives are denied opportunities for outside exposure, confined to the house, not taught how to drive a car, and not allowed a say in matters regarding the rearing of children.

Asian American preachers must give voice to the pain of Asian American women, a pain that reveals the interlocking of three "isms": sexism, racism, and classism. Rather than disown and look down upon these women, the preacher and the congregation must work together to enable these women to affirm their dignity as beings created in the image of God.

INTERNAL CONTRADICTION
WITHIN ASIAN AMERICAN COMMUNITIES

We may think that only white Americans tell Asian Americans to go home to their country of origin. Asian Americans do that to their own kind, too, when the United States is criticized. This is pervasive among Filipino Americans who have experienced colonization for centuries. It is unimaginable for many of them to criticize the United States when it is the fulfillment of their dreams; it is like vomiting one's dream. Criticism is tantamount to ungratefulness. Among some Filipino Americans, it is to be without *utang na loob* (debt of gratitude). One must take the United States, warts and all, or leave it. This is what many of them believe they can repay the United States.

Asian American perceptions of and relationship with one another also reveal elements of prejudice and social stratification. Among the most recent U.S. immigrants, for example, there is a tendency to place the social status of the following groups in this top-down order: Vietnamese, Cambodians, Laotians, and Hmongs. Generally, other Asian Americans do not like to be identified with Asian "refugees" to the United States.

It is an arduous task for Asian American preachers to raise the social awareness of their congregations that they may realize that prophetic criticism is not a betrayal of their dream, but a necessary move to realize the America of their dreams. In light of the people's internal contradictions, Asian American preachers must articulate the common plight of Asian Americans as well as point out the stereotypes and prejudices they hold against one another and other races.

AMERICA IS IN OUR HEARTS: UNFINISHED DREAM, HISTORICAL PROJECT

America is in the hearts of Asian Americans, and they have not given up the America of their dreams. They know that they have toiled in this land and have earned the right to claim their adopted country, but America is still a society unwilling to embrace its diversity. This is America's dilemma: It is the "denial of our immensely varied selves," says Ronald Takaki.[21] America, for Asian Americans, is still an "unfinished dream."

A dream is obviously not a blueprint, but it is a dream of a future in which Asians and other minorities will have their rightful place. The realization of the America of their hearts and the America of their dreams can come only through a transformative historical project. Without this historical project the America of their hearts will forever be a dream. This historical project for sure will be long and protracted, but this project has to start. For Bulosan, the task is not only to seek to understand America but also to make America a just society; it is to realize the America of his heart.[22]

Asian Americans are called to realize the America of their hearts. This is a challenge that Asian American preachers must proclaim to their congregations. Asian Americans are *Americans,* and Asian American preachers, says Jung Young Lee, must preach "not only what it means to be [an Asian], but also what it means to be an American."[23] Euro-Americans should not be left with the task of defining what it means to be an American.

LINKING EXPERIENTIAL ENTRY POINTS AND THEOLOGY

Asian American preachers-theologians are confronted with an immense deconstructive and reconstructive task of theological interpretation. Their daily contact and ministry make them the primary theological interpreters of their communities' experience. Deconstructive and reconstructive interpretation is an arena of ministry that they have to engage, for the preachers must deconstruct interpretations that are hurtful and advance interpretations that contribute to the well-being of their communities.

EXODUS CONQUEST VERSUS EXODUS EXILE

In recent years a host of writings questioned the exodus-liberation narrative as the main narrative for marginalized people in their struggle for survival and liberation. This liberating narrative, however, is simultaneously a "narrative of terror" (exodus/conquest narrative), for the acquisition of the promised land comes by way of conquest of a people (Canaanites), through the help of Yahweh, the liberator turned conqueror.

The exodus/conquest narrative, it seems to me, fits well the Euro-American experience, more than it fits the struggling peoples of the Two-Thirds World and racial/ethnic minorities in the belly of Uncle Sam. Euro-Americans made an exodus from the "old world" into the "new world" by way of conquest of the American Canaanites—the Native Americans. Oppressed peoples, however, cannot fully identify with the exodus/conquest narrative because they have not conquered a nation; instead, they are the conquered ones.[24] Asian Americans have not entered the promised land (United States) as jubilant conquerors; instead, most of them have landed on American shores as colonized peoples and have experienced life as exiles. Thus, I suggest that what suits best the Asian American experience is not an exodus/conquest narrative but exodus/exile.

The exodus/exile narrative needs further elaboration, for in the exilic land Asian Americans, through their efforts and struggles, have not only survived but also thrived and prospered. In the land of exile they have blossomed; in the new land they have learned to sing the Sovereign's song (Ps. 137); in the new land they have dreamed dreams.

The Asian American preacher must be able to articulate this journey from exodus, exile, and the relative experience of prosperity of the community. He or she must nourish them and celebrate with them in their accomplishments and joys. But she or he must remain vigilant and must not withhold prophetic words, for the newfound comforts also offer new temptations.

The Thanksgiving Sunday sermon can be an occasion to remind the congregation of their journey into the new land and the temptations with which they must wrestle. In a sermon I delivered for this occasion, I used Deuteronomy 8:11–20 as a text and lifted up a few highlights of the Israelites' journey into the promised land. The Israelites, as they were about to enter the promised land, took time to reflect about their prospects of a new life—the blessings and perils—and their calling as a people. They were also admonished to remember who they were, especially in light of Yahweh's saving activity, that in understanding who they *were* they might understand better who they *are* and who they *will be* and to whom *they belong*. Filipino Americans, like the Israelites of old, need to reflect upon the blessings and perils of their new life. Astray from the orienting center, many of them have sought security by relentlessly going after material goods and have buried their depression by buying more and consuming more.

ENCOUNTERING GOD IN ONE'S ETHNIC IDENTITY

"Trying hard to be an American," but still "falling short" of the normative American (the white Euro-American), is the plight of Asian Americans. No matter how hard Asian Americans try to be Americans, they cannot be Americans if the normative American is the white Euro-American; they will forever fall short of the norm; they will remain aberrations from the norm, forever "missing the mark" (sinners). Falling short of this norm is like falling from grace; outside this norm is hell, a place where an encounter with God is seen as impossible. Many Asian American young people, in an effort to be as American as possible and be cool, even deny their cultural and ethnic identity and, at times, blame their parents for their physical features. They want to be just like any white youth because that is the basis of getting out of the hell of nonacceptance. Whites, often with the intention of being nice, say: "We consider you to be just like us. You don't seem Asian."[25]

Can Asian Americans remain who they are and still encounter the God of Jesus? My answer is unequivocally yes. It is not simply yes, but there is no other way it can be. If a claim is made that we encounter God outside who we are, it is actually an encounter of a god that works for a foreign master. We encounter God in the context of who we are, not outside who we are. "I encountered God in my ethnicity," claims Elizabeth Tay.[26] The "self-identification of each racial and ethnic group is necessary," contends Fumitaka Matsuoka, "for the task of self-identification is a precondition to acknowledge the very nature of the gospel."[27] Moreover, self-identification is necessary for human agency and social transformation.

The tyranny of the normative race needs to be challenged and exposed as an idolatry, the deification of a certain race. Along with this unmasking of racist idolatry, preachers must strongly affirm in sermons that one's ethnic identity is a locus of encounter with the Divine. Asian American preachers have biblical resources to substantiate this point in the Jewish people's encounter with Yahweh and in God's incarnate presence in the life of the Jewish Jesus. When this ethnic identity is transgressed, as when preachers uproot Jesus and his message from his Jewish identity, the Christian gospel gets distorted. If, in the case of the Jews, the gospel of the uprooted Jewish Jesus has promoted anti-Jewish sentiments, likewise the gospel that is uprooted from the ethnic and cultural identity of Asian Americans has promoted the denial and subjugation of Asian Americans.

A COLORFUL AND COLOR-LOVING GOD

If Asian Americans encounter God in their ethnicity, this must be the God whom they can identify with and who has identified with them. Encounter with God in one's ethnicity also propels an analogous construal of who God is. As one's ethnicity is illumined in the God encounter, so also is God revealed in that encounter through the prism of one's ethnic identity. A further statement by Tay points in this direction: "My identity as an Asian American woman who has been marginalized in American culture shapes, propels and is analogous to my understanding of God."[28]

"In the eyes of God color does not matter" is a statement often heard in our pulpits. "Don't worry, brother; don't worry, sister; after all we are equal in the sight of God" is commonplace pulpit rhetoric. No matter how good the intention, I believe that it is counterproductive to preach as if color does not matter to God. The idea that color does not matter to God does not deal with the unchangeable reality that we have different colors. This approach continues to devalue the people of color's color and fails to criticize our ideological distortion: that the problem is not our differences but the way we interpret our differences.

Asian American preachers-theologians, like other preachers-theologians of color, affirm a color-loving God. In their writings and sermons they have strongly spoken of a God who affirms their color, a color that has been devalued in a white racist society. For them God is not colorless; God is colorful, and God delights in the variety of colors. Yes, God transcends colors, but God transcends not by becoming colorless; rather, God affirms the uniqueness and beauty of each color. God delights and takes cognizance of the variety of colors; for to be noncognizant of people's color is to be noncognizant of the pain of those who suffer because of their color. Thus, Asian American preachers speak of a colorful and color-loving God.

PREACHING MOTIFS AND METAPHORS
FOR BIRTHING A BETTER TOMORROW

Out of my attempt to name the pain, *han*, and hope of Asian American people, my effort to grapple with who I am and whose I am, and my wrestling to read theologically the journey of a people, a few significant motifs have come to the fore that, I believe, are helpful in preaching justice.

One motif that is expressive of Asian Americans' hope for a better tomorrow, and in contrast to Babel, is the Pentecost account. Pentecost is not Babel (confusion) but points to a society in which various cultures and races celebrate and honor their differences. Asian Americans' "visionary memory"—a vision that exhumes the past—does not point to a world where their colors are melted.[29] On the contrary, they ache and long for a colorful future. This colorful future is not, however, a mere pluralism or a multicolored world, but a world in which difference and power dynamics are taken into account. The preacher must be able to lift up this motif and affirm the value of pluralism. Preaching justice must be predicated on the vision symbolized by the Pentecost event.

In contrast to the "melting pot," another image or motif, which came out of the burning of south central Los Angeles, is conveyed in the "melting furnace."[30] The "pillar of flame" that consumed the stores of Korean Americans in south central L.A. reminds us of the "pillar of fire" (Exod. 13:21–22) that guided Moses and the Israelites toward a new tomorrow. In the L.A. "pillar of flame" God's horrendous presence was there, making us come to our senses that we are going to be consumed by the fire of racism and classism unless these "isms" are subjected to the "melting furnace." This "melting furnace" is not the melting pot of assimilation, but a furnace that burns our idols of death, purges us of our bigotry, and energizes us to continue struggling for a reconciled relationship. Out of this context and spirit Asian American preachers speak of the "fire of hope."

Asian Americans are still in an exilic journey, an image/motif very much alive in their experience. Though they have settled in this land, they still embody the exilic journey of being both insiders and outsiders; of continuously searching for their identity in a pluralistic society; of dreaming and hoping for a better tomorrow. This exilic journey is their home: in this home they have not only survived but also thrived, and in this home they have dreamed and have continued to dream.

The wrestling that I have done has also given more clarity to some urgent and unfinished tasks that Asian American preachers face. Asian American preachers have the immense task of articulating and giving voice to the *han* and hope of Asian Americans. This deep *han* that Asian American preachers are called to exhume and give voice was expressed passionately during a public hearing for American Japanese who were formerly camp internees. Poet Janice Mirikitani gives voice to this *han* in this poem to her mother, who was an internee:

> Mr. Commissioner,
> So when you tell me I must limit
> testimony,
> when you tell me my time is up,
> I tell you this:
> Pride has kept my lips
> pinned by nails
> my rage coffined. ·
> But I exhume my past
> to claim this time.[31]

Exhume the past—this is the challenge of Mirikitani to Asian American preachers, for there is no visionary memory that forgets the pains of the past. Filipino Americans have a saying: a*ng hindi lumingon sa pinangalingan ay hindi makararating sa paruruonan* (a person who does not look back at where she or he comes from cannot reach to her or his destination). To forgive and move forward is not to forget; it is to remember the *dis*membered.

Along with this exhuming of the past, Asian American preachers are called to read theologically the exilic journey of a people, and they must lift up overarching motifs and images that would nurture and provide guideposts as they move along toward the dreamed-for future.

They, with pain and lament, must also preach God's prophetic no to the idols of death within the church and the wider world without. The idols of death — racism, classism, sexism, speciesism, and so on — must pass through the melting furnace. The Christian communities must collaborate with the wider community in passing legislation to stop racist practices and similar acts, but "no government," says Lourdino Yuzon, a Filipino American preacher, "can command a people not to be racist." What is required, he says, is that a deeper internal transformation must happen.[32]

America for Asian American preachers is still an unfinished dream, and they have not given up the America of their hearts. The "pillar of fire" that they have experienced has rekindled a "fire of hope." They believe that there is and must be a tomorrow, and they have continued to dream and to actively anticipate a new tomorrow. They have not ceased to dream, to struggle, and to preach throughout all seasons until the America of their hearts has become a reality. O America, you are an unfinished dream.

CHAPTER FIVE

A Hispanic Perspective

BY THE RIVERS OF BABYLON

JUSTO L. GONZÁLEZ

WHEN I AM ASKED what is my understanding of preaching as an act of ministry, my response always emphasizes the word "act." Preaching is first and foremost an act, an event. Indeed, I am very much disturbed when people speak of a piece of paper or a manuscript as a "sermon." A sermon is not a text. A sermon is an event. In that event, the text—whether written, outlined, or completely oral—is just one element. And I am not convinced that it is always the most important element!

Then preaching as an act *of ministry* is a relationship. Ministry can never be performed alone. Nor is it ever a one-way relationship, in which one gives and another receives. In the case of preaching, this means that the "preacher" and the congregation are both constructing the sermon together as the event itself unfolds. This does not necessarily mean that the preacher improvises. It means that the sermon takes place in the encounter and the mutual interaction between the preacher's words and the congregation's response, which in many Hispanic churches may be quite verbal, and in others not.

SOCIAL LOCATION

In that relationship, social location is of great importance. Yet it is not only a matter of the social location of the preacher; it is also a matter of the social location of the congregation, and of the relationship between the two locations. I am a Cuban-born Hispanic American United Methodist with a Ph.D. and a fairly comfortable income. In different settings, and preaching in different congregations, one of these may be more important than another. Part of what I must do as I approach a preaching event—and sometimes in the midst of it—is to figure out which of these is paramount in this particular event.

As one who preaches quite often in Hispanic churches, and equally often in churches of the dominant culture, I have become very much aware that how one preaches justice depends on who the audience is. If the subject is racial justice when speaking to a predominantly white, Euro-American congregation, one is speaking mostly to those who have no firsthand experience of the negative impact of racism throughout our entire society. In that case, one's goal may be for the congregation to realize the evils of racism.

If, in contrast, one is preaching in Spanish to a Latino congregation, there is no need to tell *them* of the evil impact and the pervading nature of racism. In this case, one may feel the need to encourage the congregation in the struggle against stereotyping and other forms of racism, or to realize that there are in our society other groups that have also suffered and continue suffering the evils of racism.[1]

Justice, and preaching justice, must be seen primarily as a matter of relationships. In any situation of injustice, there is an uneven relationship, in which one party has undue rights or power over the other. Oversimplifying the matter for our present purposes, in any relationship of injustice there is a powerful party and a powerless one—or at least a relatively powerful party and a relatively powerless one.

Therefore, when preaching justice, one must take into account the situation of the congregation vis-à-vis others. Are they the powerful who must repent of their injustice, or are they the powerless who must be encouraged to claim their rights? Are they to repent of having abused their power (which is most commonly the sin of the powerful) or of not having used whatever power they had (which is most commonly the sin of the powerless)? Quite clearly, it will not do to tell the powerful that they must lay claim to their power and try to increase it. Nor will it do to tell the powerless that they must relinquish whatever measure of power they have. It will not do to tell those who already think too highly of themselves that they ought to lay claim to the image of God that is in them, and thus to be more proud of who they are. Nor will it do to tell the powerless whose self-image has been defaced by constant injustice and stereotyping that they ought not to think too highly of themselves.

To complicate matters further, the "powerful" and the "powerless" are such only in relative terms and within the parameters of a given relationship. Thus, I may be preaching to a woman who, as a Latina, suffers the injustices of a racist society. Yet she has attained sufficient authority in her job that she has several subordinates whom she may be tempted to oppress. At home, she may be an abused wife, oppressed by a husband who is physically more powerful than she is.

In consequence, when I preach justice, I must do it in such a fashion that the unjust relationships to which I am referring are very clear, and if people find themselves in other unjust relationships, they realize that what I am saying does not transfer directly to the other relationships without first determining their role in them. For instance, if I speak in a Hispanic congregation about the racial and cultural oppression of Latinos in this society and church, and I call my audience to be more forceful and not allow others to determine their lives and their future, I must make it very clear to the abusing husbands in my congregation that in the case of their family relationships the prescription is another—that the shoe is on the other foot, and the affirming message is not for them, but for their wives.

Another way to speak of the same issues is to conceive of a relationship in terms of center and periphery. Those at the center are the powerful ones, the ones who make decisions that affect both center and periphery, the ones who find it easiest to commit injustice. Those at the periphery are the powerless ones, those who are most often exploited by the center, and whose lives are in great measure determined by decisions made at the center, often without taking them into consideration. What complicates matters, however, is that there is not just one center and one periphery. Society—and church—is polycentric. It is very much like a complex galaxy in which moons revolve around planets, planets around stars, stars around other stars, and so on to the point that even the minutest particle and the largest sun are both center and periphery.

Similar relationships come into play with regard to the preacher and who she or he is. As a Latino preacher, I have been acutely aware during most of my preaching career that I am perceived and received differently in a Euro-American than in a Hispanic congregation. These preconceptions have to do with two matters: my authority and my subject.

My authority varies according to the congregation to which I am preaching. Even within Latino circles, this is true. If I am presented as a guest preacher in a United Methodist Hispanic congregation (my own denomination), I do not find that I have to prove my authority. It has been given to me by agencies whom my audience acknowledges—an Annual Conference, a Board of the Ministry, a bishop. Thus, I can approach the pulpit with confidence that people expect me to speak to them the Word of God. In some Hispanic pentecostal congregations, however, I found in years past (before I became better known to them) that I had to prove my right to be in that pulpit. I had to prove it by such unwritten and nebulous means as my use of Scripture, my style, my manner, and so forth—but I had to prove it. Such congregations expected a United Methodist preacher to be "frío"—literally, "cold," but actually meaning unanointed by the Spirit. Therefore, if I had a written text, it meant that I did not trust the Spirit; if I was not ready to follow the flow of their responses to my words, I was bound by the letter that kills; if I did not speak of my own experience with God, I had none.

The same is generally the experience of ethnic minority preachers when they walk to the pulpit of a predominantly white, Euro-American congregation. All sorts of stereotypes are at work. If I tell a joke, this proves that Latinos are frivolous and incapable of responsible commitment. If I am too serious, this shows that Latinos tend to be fanatical and even superstitious. If I have an accent that is not North European, then I probably do not really know what I am talking about—unless I confine myself to quaint stories about my people. If I show that I know what I am talking about, either because my sermon demonstrates it or because I have credentials to prove it, then I am not a real Latino, and my presence there simply shows that even among us there are exceptions.

Clearly, what I have just said is something of an exaggeration. The truth is that there is in the Christian community sufficient goodwill—I would rather say, that the Holy Spirit is so active in our communities—that no matter what the general stereotypes may be that people bring to listening to a sermon, the Word of God can break through, and we can have an encounter with God that goes beyond, and corrects, our refusals to encounter one another. But even though an exaggeration, it is generally true, and must be said clearly and plainly, so that we may undo its consequences.

Then the perceptions of people have to do not only with my person, but also with my subject. When I preach in a Hispanic congregation, people in general expect me to preach the gospel. Today I may put special emphasis on a matter of justice, and tomorrow on one of stewardship. But in general, people do not expect that because of who I am, they already know what I am going to speak about.

That is not generally the case in a Euro-American congregation. Unfortunately, for many years, when a preacher of color preached in a white church, the subject was always race relations. It was taken for granted that on any other subject, the norm was a white preacher. But on Race Relations Sunday, on Martin Luther King Jr. Day, or on any other occasion when it appeared particularly appropriate to speak of race and racism, the preacher was a person of color. In the case of Hispanics and Latin Americans, if the subject was not race and racism, then it was international and economic justice. Therefore, it is not surprising that when a person of color preaches as a guest in a white congregation, people expect the subject to be justice.

For that reason, as a preacher of justice, I find it necessary to make it very clear that I am not a preacher of my own interests or pet subjects, but a preacher of the Word.

PREACHING IN THE LATINO COMMUNITY

As I have said, I preach about half the time in the Hispanic/Latino community, and the other half in churches of the dominant culture. Also, only about one-third of these preaching occasions are in churches of my denomination (United Methodist). During the last year, for instance, I have preached in churches of several mainline Protestant denominations, as well as Roman Catholic, evangelical, pentecostal, and Seventh-Day Adventist churches. I have also attended a wide variety of churches. Therefore, I am quite reluctant to speak of preaching "in the Latino community" in general, as if there were not a great variety of theological and social settings within that community. In fact, just about every homiletical and hermeneutical school in the Euro-American tradition has its counterpart in the Hispanic community.

Still, when it comes to the general subject of this book, I dare say that one hears much less preaching about "justice" in the Latino community than one does in the Euro-American community. For an Anglo observer, this may seem strange. Are we not among the people in this society who most often suffer economic and social injustice? Are we not underrepresented in all the decision-making circles of church and society? Yes. And that is precisely why we do not feel the need to preach justice in our churches.

For us, the gospel is a word of justice. God's eternal purposes are purposes of justice. The reign of God is a reign of justice. Therefore, when we speak of the familial bonds that are created in baptism, we speak about justice. When we speak of the Parousia, we speak about justice. When we speak of stewardship, we speak about justice. (We certainly do not take for granted, as do most Anglo preachers on stewardship, that everything anyone has, has been given by God to manage. Perhaps it has been stolen! Perhaps, even though legally acquired, it is the result of injustice!)

In short, we do not need to speak constantly about justice because the constant experience of our people is one of injustice, and therefore the good news is necessarily a word of justice.

INJUSTICE AND THE HISPANIC/LATINO COMMUNITY

The experience of injustice is constant within the Latino community. It is injustice both in our relationship with the rest of society and within our community. Both are so obvious that a few words will suffice.

First, as to injustice vis-à-vis the society at large, for the last three decades, in census after census, in almost every negative statistic, Hispanic figures have remained at a constant of one and a half times the figure for the entire country. Thus, for instance, when unemployment is at 6 percent, Latino unemployment is at 9 percent. If unemployment rises to 10 percent, ours goes to 15 percent. When the poverty rate is 20 percent in the society at large, in the Hispanic community it is 30 percent. The same is true of statistics having to do with school dropouts, inadequate housing, incarceration, and so forth.

Added to these economic signs of injustice are discrimination and prejudice at all levels. There are people in California and Texas whose ancestors have lived in those areas for five or six generations, and they are still made to feel as foreigners and even asked why they do not go home. (Actually, even the present rhetoric about immigration ignores the fact that roughly 75 percent of all Hispanics in the United States are citizens by birth, and not immigrants.) It is not necessary to go far to find injustice in the manner the Hispanic community is treated by the rest of society.

Then there is also injustice within our own communities. There is sexual injustice, often manifested by spousal abuse. There is economic injustice, in that some Hispanics who have a little more than others use that as a means to gain advantage and to exploit the others. There is injustice in the relationships among various waves of immigrants and among people of different national origins.

Our people are well acquainted with injustice. And precisely for this reason, Hispanic preaching at its best does not need to mention justice constantly, as if it were not a known goal among our people. We do need (1) to refer to the injustices that take place among ourselves, and that are often eclipsed by the injustice perpetrated on us, and (2) to relate every aspect of the gospel, every doctrine, every act of worship, every act of preaching, to the yearning for justice that already exists within our people. This is not the same as preaching justice within the context of a Euro-American congregation that has little notion—or at least little firsthand experience—of the injustice that it inflicts on minorities and others.

RECONSTRUCTING THEOLOGY

Lest we be too optimistic, it is necessary to say that the Hispanic church community still has to go a long way before it rids itself of much theological baggage that it has received from elsewhere, and that impedes its dealings with issues of justice and injustice. Hispanic Protestantism is mostly the result of North American missionary work, and such missionary work generally coincided with the high point of the ideology of Manifest Destiny. Thus, historically, Hispanic Protestantism has viewed North American society as a paragon to be imitated rather than criticized. And this tendency has been reinforced by a theology, inherited from that missionary enterprise, that sees very little connection between doctrine and justice.

The result is that a vast task of theological deconstruction and reconstruction faces the Latino community. Indeed, the last ten years have seen an explosion of Hispanic theology attempting such reconstruction, from the doctrine of God to eschatology, and including such items as the doctrine of the Trinity, anthropology, Christology, soteriology, and so forth. Significantly, this literature has gained wide acceptance among Latino preachers and is making a significant impact on the Latino pulpit. This literature is too vast and far-reaching to summarize here. However, it would not be an exaggeration to say that a new, widely ecumenical, Hispanic theology is developing in the United States—a theology that unfortunately is still generally unknown to the rest of the Christian community.

THE WORD OF JUSTICE

One element that has become quite clear to many Hispanic preachers and theologians is that preaching is not just a two-way relationship between a congregation and a preacher. There is also a third element, and one that most Hispanic preachers consider normative: the Scriptures. Ultimately, we do not preach justice because we suffer injustice. We preach justice because we preach the Word of God, and that is a word of justice.

This distinction is important. If our preaching of justice were based solely on our experience of injustice, then we, the preachers, would be making ourselves masters of the Word. We might as well preach recreation because we are bored. No; we preach justice because we preach the Word. As preachers, in the preaching event we are part of a triangle: preacher-congregation-Scripture. The relationship that I began describing at the beginning of this chapter must also include this third element, and that third element must be given its freedom to be itself. We do not decide that our community needs justice and then seek a passage of scripture that deals with the subject. On the contrary, it is in allowing the Word to speak freely that we discover the word of justice.

When preaching to Euro-American congregations, I find it necessary to make this very clear. For that reason, when preaching in such congregations, I never select the obvious passages that deal with justice. Were I to stand at a pulpit, with the intention of showing the centrality of justice in God's will for us, and begin by saying, "The text I have chosen for this morning is from the prophet Amos," those who most need to hear my sermon would immediately decide that they know what I am going to say and turn me off. If I insist on preaching on Amos and James, with an occasional use of the harsher passages in Isaiah or Jeremiah, they would be justified in turning me off, for by selecting the passages from which I preach and insisting on passages that clearly make my point, I would have made myself master, and not servant, of the Word. And that is in itself an unjust relationship!

If justice is, as I believe it is, central to the message of the Bible, then it will come forth, no matter what the text. I do not have to manipulate the selection of texts so as to preach only from those that are easy and obvious. On the contrary, any text, when properly opened and listened to, will convey a message of justice.

Thus, my resistance to selecting texts from James or Amos is both a matter of strategy and a matter of theological conviction. As a strategy, it makes it impossible for the most recalcitrant in the congregation to say, "Here we go again," and refuse to listen even before I have begun to speak. As a matter of theology, such resistance is grounded on my conviction that justice is so central to the biblical message that it appears everywhere, and if we see it only in the most explicit passages, it is because we have ruled it out of our theology to such a point that it is now a marginal and occasional subject, to be preached only on Race Relations Sunday or when Amos comes up in the lectionary.

THE WORD INTERPRETED

How, then, does one interpret a biblical passage so that the justice issues present in it come to the foreground? Quite unconsciously, I have developed—or rather, have learned from other preachers who used it equally unconsciously—a method that could be called "correlation."[2] That is, I explore the relationships of power and powerlessness that appear in the text and then seek parallelisms with similar relationships in our society. This method expresses a similarity rather than an exact proportionality, an applicability to our situation rather than an automatic, necessary, exact mathematical conclusion, and it can be applied differently according to different circumstances.

Let us take one example. In Hebrews 11:24–25 we read: "By faith Moses, when he was grown up, refused to be called a son of Pharaoh's daughter, choosing rather to share ill-treatment with the people of God than to enjoy the fleeting pleasures of sin." In this case, we are told that Moses had a choice. He could be part of the power elite of Egypt, or he could identify with the people of God. Before he opts for the people of God, he is part of the elite. Thereafter, he is part of the oppressed. Thus, the question of power and powerlessness does not refer only to two different persons or two groups, but also to two options of a potentially powerful individual.

Now suppose I am preaching to a Latino congregation where people are upwardly mobile, which is quite often the case in our churches. They, too, have the option to move up, to become part of the elite, or to cast their lot with their own people. Thus, I can draw two stages of correlation. First, I may show the parallelism between the children of Israel in Egypt and our own people in whatever circumstance we now find ourselves. But then I may draw a further parallelism, which comes to be the challenge of the text: Just as Moses had to make a choice, and faith led him to opt for the children of Israel, so do you, my listener, have to make a choice, and faith calls you to opt for the downtrodden of today rather than for success as the world understands it.

From that point, I can make other connections between the two situations. I may do this by discussing how the situation played out in the life of Moses, as seen in the next two verses in Hebrews: "He considered abuse suffered for the Christ to be greater wealth than the treasures of Egypt, for he was looking ahead to the reward. By faith he left Egypt, unafraid of the king's anger; for he persevered as though he saw him who is invisible" (vv. 26–27).

Here a number of secondary correlations come into play. On the one hand, there are wealth and the treasures of Egypt. On the other, abuse and fear. Moses considered abuse better than wealth, and he was unafraid of the anger of the most powerful king of his time. Why? Because he had faith. My listener can then be prepared to pay the price in abuse and fear of the option that I am proposing, and may see that this is possible only through a faith that perseveres as if seeing the invisible.

A second example may illustrate how this works in a passage that is not often considered in regard to justice. In Acts 6:1–6 is the story usually called the election of the seven deacons. The text never calls them deacons—but that is another matter. In any case, the text begins with an unjust relationship—real or perceived. The widows of the "Hellenists" apparently are not receiving as much in the distribution of help by the church as the widows of the "Hebrews." This parallels Palestinian Jewish society in the first century, where the "Hebrew" Jews were considered superior and more religious than the "Hellenistic" Jews. Thus we have a situation of inequality in society. This unjust societal relationship, for whatever reasons, has now made its way into the church and its treatment of the widows (actually, in the manner in which the apostles treat them, for they are the ones in charge of the distribution). Thus, the arrangement that causes difficulties is the difference between how the apostles treat the "Hebrew" widows and how they treat the "Hellenistic" widows. So far, nothing has changed, and the church seems to be an organization like any other. But then the seven are selected who will henceforth control the distribution. What group do they represent? Their names are all Greek, and therefore it appears clear that at least the majority, if not the entirety, are "Hellenistic" Jews (one of them is not even a born Jew, but a convert). Thus, the church's action introduces a radical discontinuity. What has taken place here is a radical shift, so that those who have experienced powerlessness and neglect will now be in charge of the distribution to *all* segments of the church.

Applying now the method of "correlation of relationships," one could begin by asking where in our society one finds inequalities parallel to those expressed in the text. Suppose that we are dealing with cultural and ethnic inequalities; one would begin by exploring the correlations between the tendency to exclude "Hellenists" from "good" Jewish circles and the manner in which this society views Hispanics. For instance, in Palestine the "Hellenistic" Jews were considered outsiders, in part because they had not been born there, in part because their food and their customs were different, in part because they spoke a different language, and when they spoke the local Aramaic, they did so with an accent, and so forth.

All of these elements find their parallelism in the experience of being Hispanic in the United States. Then one could develop the parallelism further by exploring how this works out in the church. In the church in Jerusalem, when it came to the distribution to the widows, the unequal relationship in society was reflected inside the church. Is this true today? If we substitute pastors or congregations for the widows, can we say that today's ethnic pastors and congregations, as compared to the majority pastors and congregations, are treated with an inequality similar to what the early church practiced among its widows? And finally, if this is true, the sermon would explore what it would mean for today's church to act as the church in Jerusalem did.

Still on the same passage, and to illustrate how the same texts may deal with a number of injustices, the preacher may point out that the apostles decided that seven *men* be elected, and that they would not preach but manage the finances of the church. Yet in the very next verse, we are told that Stephen, one of the seven, began preaching. Eventually, Stephen, who according to the apostles was not supposed to be preaching at all, ends up preaching the longest sermon in the entire book of Acts! Could it not be that the same Spirit who in some measure supported the decision of the church, but also in some measure surprised them by giving Stephen (and then Philip) a job description far beyond what the Twelve had allowed for them, is now surprising the church by pointing out that such offices cannot be limited to men?

Finally, take as an example a text that apparently has nothing to do with justice. In Luke 13:6–9 we read:

> Then he told this parable: "A man had a fig tree planted in his vineyard; and he came looking for fruit on it and found none. So he said to the gardener, 'See here! For three years I have come looking for fruit on this fig tree, and still I find none. Cut it down! Why should it be wasting the soil?' He replied, 'Sir, let it alone for one more year, until I dig around it and put manure on it. If it bears fruit next year, well and good; but if not, you can cut it down.'"

There are several ways in which this parable may be approached following the method here proposed. For instance, one could approach it on the basis of the relationship between the owner of the vineyard and the gardener. But one may also approach it in terms of the place of the fig tree in the midst of the vineyard. The gardener and the owner (and we, who have been let into the secret) know that the fig tree is not very productive. But a passerby, looking at the vineyard at the time of the year when this dialogue would take place (when the last chance of a fig crop had passed, and the vineyard was already pruned), would see a verdant fig tree in the midst of the gnarled and apparently unproductive stumps of the vines. Thus, one could say that from the perspective of those "not in the know," the fig tree is privileged, and the vines are not. This is even reinforced by the gardener's attention, digging around the fig tree and providing it with additional fertilizer.

From the perspective of the owner and the gardener, however, the reality is very different. The fig tree receives special attention precisely because it is so unproductive. And if it does not respond to that special attention, its fate is sealed. Thus, the parable brings in a temporal line, a future that may be hidden to casual observers, but has already been decided by the owner and the gardener. The fig tree has been given the position of privilege; but if it does not produce, it will be utterly destroyed—a point that is made clearer by the context immediately preceding the parable, in which Jesus speaks of people who have died apparently for no reason and tells his hearers, "Unless you repent, you will likewise perish." The present superiority of the fig tree over the vines is only apparent and temporary. The vines have been pruned so that they may produce more fruit. The fig tree has been allowed to grow with the hope that it might at least begin to produce something.

If we were now to bring the fig tree/vine relationship to bear on today's relationships, it is apparent that in our society many persons seem never to be pruned. They live in ease. They have all that is needed for a comfortable life—and more. And there are others (many of them in our ethnic minority churches) who seem to be constantly pruned. They are frequently unemployed; and when they are employed, their wages are barely sufficient to meet their most basic needs. They seem to have been forgotten by society, by fortune, and perhaps even by God. Yet when it comes to works of love and faithfulness to the gospel, some of these people are among the most productive. Thus, if preaching to the prosperous (and particularly to those who think that it suffices to contribute a minimal part of their income to charity, and that with that they have given sufficient fruit), the preacher may need to point out to them that there is a correlation between their situation and that of the fig tree in the parable. You may appear privileged; but if you do not repent and produce fruit of mercy, you will not survive.

THE FALSE CONSCIOUSNESS OF POWER

It is very difficult for middle-class North Americans—and even more so for white male middle-class North Americans—to declare themselves powerless. Perhaps the greatest obstacle that a preacher of justice finds when preaching to Euro-American middle-class congregations—and sometimes also to Hispanic and other ethnic minority middle-class congregations—is a false image of power that this society fosters. Indeed, the basic mythology of this society is so steeped in this false image that it is one of the most difficult illusions to destroy.

In our society, power is one of the main indicators of success. Whoever lacks power is considered a failure. The very notion of democracy is based on the unstated assumption that all voters have a measure of power—a power that they then partly delegate to their elected officials. Thus, those who do not have power must have done something wrong; they must have failed in their responsibilities or be somehow deficient in ability or character. For this reason, it is absolutely imperative for middle-class people (particularly middle-class men) to cling to the illusion of power. One may not have as much power as the president of the United States or the CEO of a great corporation; but one's worth is still vindicated in that one has a measure of power to determine one's life—where and how one will live, how one will spend one's money, and so forth. Furthermore, the manner in which the system assures the support of the middle class is by allowing it the measure of power it has (and also by allowing it to fancy that it has more power and freedom than it really does).[3]

A further obstacle lies in the manner in which North American culture has remythologized the nature of evil. In more traditional views, evil was often personalized in the depiction of a devil with tail, horns, and pitchfork. Having debunked that myth, the most common North American myth depicts evil as simply something we have created, and we can therefore control if we simply set our minds to the task. Evil has no real power, except what we give it. In a way, this is the extreme expression of our fear of powerlessness, for we would rather see ourselves as creators and masters of evil than as captives in bondage to it. If we have the power to master it— even if we do not apply that power—evil is not so bad after all.

For this reason, the preacher of justice often finds that it is quite easy to foster a sense of guilt in middle-class congregations. By feeling guilty, people retain their sense of power. They have done the injustice or at least have failed to use their power to stop it. Their vision of the order of society and of their place in it is not radically altered. All that is required to do justice is to repent of that one item in which one has been unjust and to use one's power for justice. Significantly, after one of these frequent experiences that could literally be called guilt *trips*, little changes. The listeners go back to life as before, except that now they have a lingering sense of guilt. They retain their sense of power, the illusion that if they really wished to do so, they could fix whatever is wrong.

The result of this sort of preaching justice, and of this reaction of guilt, is that ultimately very little changes. Here and there an individual may be moved to write a letter to a congressperson or to give a particularly liberal offering to a food program; but the system itself, which makes that individual feel powerful and then guilty for having power, is hardly challenged.

Therefore, one of the most challenging tasks of a preacher of justice in a middle-class congregation—be it Euro-American, Latina, or of any other race or culture—is to lead members of the congregation to accept the fact that they are not as powerful as they think they are. While in some of the relationships described here they are in the position of power, there are others in which they are powerless. Indeed, in many cases their own unrecognized powerlessness vis-à-vis the entire system makes it very difficult for them not to abuse their power vis-à-vis those who are even more powerless.

The preacher of justice in such a setting must not be content with making the congregation feel guilty for the injustices they commit. The preacher of justice must lead the congregation to understand that they are in a position in which much of their privilege and supposed power is gained at the expense of their accepting the present order of things, and thus becoming powerless to do much about the deepest injustices in our society. By coming to realize and to accept their powerlessness, they can begin to be in real and effective solidarity with the other powerless people in whose oppression they partake. Such solidarity will then go beyond acts of charity and will seek ways to alter the system itself that oppresses them and those whose poverty, exclusion, and oppression are much more obvious.

THE CHURCH AND THE REIGN OF GOD

Perhaps one way to move beyond the sort of preaching of justice that is in truth preaching of guilt is to recover the biblical notion of the reign of God. Unfortunately, liberal theologians of past decades have convinced us that eschatological belief and preaching are necessarily escapist and irrelevant. History alone suffices to disprove that notion, for almost without exception the most radical and revolutionary movements in the history of Christianity have also had a strong eschatological vision.

It is true that if by "eschatology" we mean what has often passed for the Christian hope, namely, a vision of disembodied souls floating around in clouds and cute little angels playing harps, then eschatology is indeed escapist. But that is not what Christian eschatology is all about. Christian eschatology is about a reign of God that is also a reign of justice (for God is not only love; God is also just). It is about a reign of God where "they shall all sit under their own vines and under their own fig trees, and no one shall make them afraid" (Mic. 4:4). It is about this reign that God promises: "I will seek the lost, and I will bring back the strayed, and I will bind up the injured, and I will strengthen the weak, but the fat and the strong I will destroy. I will feed them with justice" (Ezek. 34:16). Or as the book of Revelation puts it,

> They will hunger no more, and thirst no more;
>> the sun will not strike them,
>> nor any scorching heat;
> for the Lamb at the center of the throne will be their shepherd,
>> and he will guide them to springs of the water of life,
>> and God will wipe away every tear from their eyes. (Rev. 7:16–17)

These visions may seem romantic hallucinations to some; but they are precisely the visions that have sustained the church through the ages in its quest for justice, and the main source from which a preacher and a congregation may draw strength for a struggle that often appears endless and even pointless.

Yet the vision is not enough. And the words of the preacher are not enough. As Christians, we must now and then have a glimpse, however distant, of the justice that is to be. We need confirmation from other Christians that this is indeed our faith—a faith on which we are ready to stake our lives. That is why the preaching and the living of justice ultimately come back to the congregation and to the church at large. If in the community of believers we are not ready to order our lives as those who do indeed believe the visions of Micah, Ezekiel, and John of Patmos, then we might as well quit claiming those visions for ourselves. And the opposite is also true: when the community of faith lives out the justice it proclaims, its message becomes believable. Read again the book of Acts, and you will note that every time the church does something that orders its life according to the vision of the reign of God, its impact on the surrounding community is mentioned. Three passages in Acts come to mind. The first is in Acts 2, where immediately after describing in verse 46 the manner in which the early Christian community lived in love and justice, the narrator adds in verse 47: "And day by day [God] added to their number those who were being saved." The second is in Acts 5:14, where the apostles defy the unjust command of the council to be silent, "Yet more than ever believers were added to the [Sovereign], great numbers of both men and women." The third is in Acts 6, where immediately after the act of justice discussed earlier, when the early church named seven Hellenists to oversee the daily distribution, and as a result "the word of God continued to spread; the number of the disciples increased greatly in Jerusalem, and a great many of the priests became obedient to the faith" (v. 7).

Although the justice we seek and preach is not only justice for and within the church, but justice in and for all of God's creation, any effective preaching of justice has to be accompanied by the doing of justice in and by the congregation. At the beginning of this chapter, we discussed the relationship between preacher and congregation. That relationship goes far beyond what was described there. The congregation is not just the receptor of the message; it is also the mold into which it will be cast. If the congregation (and the church at large) does not practice love and justice within itself, it will never be able to hear or to believe the message of the justice of God's reign. The congregation shapes the sermon and its reception just as much as (or more than) the preacher does. The congregation is the hermeneutical community through which the interpretation of both text and sermon must pass. Thus, if the preaching of justice is not presented in such a way that the members of the congregation recognize themselves as the people of God to whom the Word is addressed, and as the people of God who are practicing obedience to God's Word, all preaching of justice is in vain. It may make some members of the congregation proud of "the prophetic preacher we have." It may make some angry at a preacher who seems to be meddling in their lives, as well as in politics and economics. It may make the preacher famous or infamous, admired or despised. But it will not bring many much closer to the reign of God.

All of which is to say that preaching, like justice, is a matter of community; therefore, the preaching of justice must also be an expression of a community committed to justice.

SPECIFIC HISPANIC IMAGES AND CORRELATIONS

The foregoing deals primarily with general issues of power and powerlessness, yet each oppressed group in a society has particular images that it finds significant. These may be different for each situation, and each group must find them for itself. For the African American community, for instance, images of slavery and deliverance are paramount, as may be seen in the traditional spirituals and in more recent black theology.

Such images are not only the particular concerns and interests of an oppressed group, but may well prove to be one of that group's main contributions to the church at large in its hermeneutical task. The African American emphasis on slavery-deliverance, and therefore on the liberation from the yoke of Egypt and the crossing of the Red Sea, has proven to be a significant insight for the entire church. Likewise, other such emphases on the part of particular groups may be seen as hermeneutical insights to be shared with the church at large — although never entirely relinquished, for in that case we lose our identity and our particular hermeneutical stance.

I have explored some of those images for Latinos and Latinas elsewhere, and I have attempted to show how they illumine the biblical text.[4] Here, I must be content with mentioning them rather briefly, so that the reader may be aware of them and recognize them as the occasion arises.

One of these images has to do with our reality as a "race" that is not a race. Living in a society where race is paramount, we are classified as a race. Yet some of us are of European descent, some of Amerindian, some of African, a few of Asian, and most of several of these in all sorts of proportions and combinations. Thus, *mestizaje* (being a mixture of European and Indian)[5] and *mulatez* (being a mixture of African and European) are ways in which we express our experience of in-betweenness. In a racist society, not only are we forced to define ourselves as a race, which we usually would not, but we are also made to feel as in-between people, as people who are neither fish nor fowl, or as it is commonly put in our circles, as people who live in the space between "accepted" definitions (Mexican American, Cuban American, and so forth). This in-betweenness leads us to focus on other in-between people in Scripture, such as the Galileans, the Samaritans, and the Gibeonites, and to seek to discover their role in the history of salvation and of the world.[6] This may be a correction to much biblical hermeneutics, which takes for granted a simple dichotomy between Jew and Gentile, and therefore misses some of the nuances, for instance, of the Galilean or the Samaritan.

Another set of images that are central to us have to do with place and belonging: exile, alienness, pilgrimage. Just as the African American sings and thinks about Israel in Egypt, so do we think of Israel in Babylon. For a number of reasons, many of us are in lands far from those of our birth. No matter how eagerly we devote ourselves to building houses and planting gardens (Jer. 29:5), we must still sing "by the rivers of Babylon" (Ps. 137:1). Others of us were born in these lands, but are well aware that when we become too visible, or when our words or our attitudes are not popular, someone will speak to us the words of Amaziah: "Flee [to your own land], earn your bread there, and prophesy there" (Amos 7:12). For these reasons, we are very much aware of the character of the Christian life as a pilgrimage in a land that is never ours, in which we must retain our memory as aliens, no matter how settled (Exod. 23:29; Lev. 19:34; Deut. 14:29; Heb. 11:9–16). And this has practical implications for issues of economic justice, for as aliens, we know that property rights are never absolute (Lev. 25:23).

Third, we resonate to images of language and culture—especially of language and culture despised and vindicated. We read the account of Pentecost as God's final "No!" to any notions of "Aramaic only"—and to any similar notions in more recent times. (Note that on that occasion, the hearers were not made to understand the language of the apostles, but the apostles were made to speak in the multitude of languages of the hearers.) We read the story of Peter being recognized as a follower of Jesus by his foreign accent (Matt. 26:73), and we come to the realization that the issues involved in the trial and crucifixion of Jesus were not merely religious, but also ethnic and political. And how often have we been excluded or mocked by many a "Shibboleth" that we could not pronounce correctly (Judg. 12:6)?

These images, however, are not our creation out of whole cloth. They are biblical images to which we resonate, in which we find ourselves. They are important to us because we find ourselves in them. But we are also convinced that they are significant for the entire church because we find them in the Bible. Thus, as we interpret Scripture and seek to make the sort of correlations described here, we frequently find ourselves asking who in the text is displaced, alien, exiled; who, although living on their native land, are made to feel as if they do not belong, as if they should have a land elsewhere. And for similar reasons, we are fascinated by stories of immigration, of crossing the river Jordan dry-shod (and dry-backed!), of seeking to create a nation out of a series of scattered tribes and clans, of protests against the mighty of the land who wish to keep all the wealth to themselves and their kin, of laws made by the powerful for others to obey.

The result of all of this is that preaching in the Hispanic community is lively. Yet it is not lively because preachers know how to enliven their sermons or because they use one particular rhetorical device or another. It is lively because in it we encounter the living Word of God; because that Word engages our very lives in their deepest hopes and hurts; because were it not for this preaching and the Word it conveys, our bones would be dried up. It is lively because a sermon is not a text, but that almost unspeakable miracle in which the preacher, the congregation, and the Word of God engage one another in a never-ending conversation.

CHAPTER SIX

A Korean American Perspective

SINGING A NEW SONG IN
A STRANGE LAND

EUNJOO MARY KIM

I GREW UP LISTENING to Christian preaching in various Protestant churches in Korea, including Presbyterian, Methodist, and Holiness churches. Although I heard sermons from different denominations, they were quite similar. They contributed to the increase of my literal knowledge of the Bible, the formation of my personal morality, and my spiritual relationship with God.

The children's sermons I heard during my childhood were stories about biblical persons asserting that God rewarded and punished them on the basis of their moral behavior. They also emphasized spiritual disciplines of memorization of Bible verses and the daily practice of prayer and Bible reading. On the one hand, this type of preaching gave me literal knowledge of the Bible and acclimated me to the devotional practices of Christianity. On the other hand, this preaching did not satisfy my intellectual curiosity about the Bible, nor did it answer sufficiently my fundamental questions about the Christian faith.

During my adolescent years, from the 1970s through the mid-1980s, the sermons I heard from the Korean church emphasized positive thinking and faith. In those days, under the dictatorships of the Park and the Chun governments, Koreans underwent intense industrialization. They were forced to sacrifice individual subjectivity and identity for the fulfillment of the national goal of economic growth. As a result, Koreans were suffering from psychological instability, political and social insecurity, and spiritual emptiness.

For those experiencing these stressful economic and political conditions, the Korean church offered a series of revival movements. That is, some world-wide revivalists such as Billy Graham were invited to the revival meetings, where the preaching centered on born-again faith or "decisions for Christ" as the essence of Christian faith. Thousands of Korean Christians gathered, from all denominations, to listen to these sermons.

At the same time, Rev. Yong-Gee Cho's preaching greatly appealed to the Korean Christians who were suffering from economic poverty, physical or mental illness, failure in business, or psychological depression and despair.[1] His preaching promised the key to succeeding in this world and to experiencing an ecstatic spiritual experience such as being slain in the "Spirit" or speaking in tongues.

Many Korean churches were influenced by this kind of spiritual movement. They held revival meetings for their congregations as often as they could and tried to give their members the opportunity to experience born-again faith and moments of spiritual ecstasy. The revivalists' messages centered on repenting for personal moral sins and making a decision to accept Christ Jesus as one's personal Savior.

The preaching of born-again faith and personal success gave temporary relief and courage to cope with the future for listeners who were under political and economic stress. However, the more I listened to those messages, the more I questioned what the essence of the Christian gospel really was. Such messages seemed to me unable to answer my fundamental questions about Christian faith, for example, the meaning of the cross and the suffering of the righteous in the world. Observing the students' movements against the dictatorship and watching the suffering of the righteous for the sake of national justice and peace, I questioned why Korean preaching emphasized a personal relationship with God and individual success, while neglecting to address the will of God for our social situation. How was it possible for Christians to enjoy their blessed lives, ignoring the unjust reality around them?

The questions I raised about Korean preaching during my youth challenged me to study Christianity at the academic level. My theological study in Korea and in the United States helped me to reflect critically and contextually from the Reformed theological perspective on the Korean and Korean American churches and their preaching.

The Korean American church has played a major role in Korean immigrant society. Historically speaking, it was born with the Korean immigrant community. After the Korean-American Treaty of Amity and Trade was signed in 1882, as the first official relationship between Korea and the United States, American missionaries encouraged those who had been converted to Christianity to go to Hawaii as a means of escaping poverty. As a result, ninety-three contract laborers came to Hawaii to the sugar and pineapple plantations as the first Korean immigrant group. When they arrived in Honolulu early in 1903, they immediately established a church in July of that year, which became the center of social and community affairs as well as the place of worship.[2]

Since the 1965 Immigration and Naturalization Act, Korean immigrants who were classified as professional have increased. Several factors contributed to the increase in Korean immigrants to the United States: the relaxed U.S. immigration law, political repression and socioeconomic instability in Korea, and the Korean government's policy of encouraging emigration. In 1990, approximately 929,533 Koreans were residing in the United States, over 80 percent of whom arrived after 1965.[3]

Korean immigrants have organized churches to meet the need for a religious and ethnic community. This practice has grown so rapidly that by 1989 there were more than three thousand Korean American churches.[4] According to statistics, almost 70 percent of the Korean immigrant population identify themselves as Christians, and 83.5 percent attend church at least once a week.[5] An interesting point is that the majority of them became churchgoers after their immigration to the United States.[6]

Korean American preaching has greatly influenced the Korean immigrant community by giving it direction. Because it is so influential, reflecting on the practice of Korean American preaching in the context of the Korean immigrant community is crucial. The renewal of Korean American preaching depends on such self-awareness. Toward this end, we need, first of all, to understand Protestant preaching from the perspective of Reformed theology.

THE UNDERSTANDING OF PREACHING

Based on my preaching experience as a pastor in a Korean American church and my experience of teaching about preaching in a Reformed seminary, I understand preaching to be an eschatological event. It is eschatological in the sense that the essence of Christian preaching is based on God's future promise of a new heaven and a new earth. The promise of God is confirmed by the Christological events of the life, death, resurrection, and second coming of Jesus Christ. Preaching helps to accomplish God's promise for us.

The nature and function of preaching can be explained in three respects. First, preaching as an eschatological event is contextual. It presupposes that

God's work is not revealed uniformly in all situations but accommodates itself to diverse situations with varying capacity. On the one hand, it reflects the concrete reality of the listener's situation with critical insights and relativizes the dehumanizing elements within the existing order and power of the world. On the other hand, it visualizes the reign of God for a particular community of faith and describes a new world in which people enjoy their restored relationship with God and with others. Eschatological preaching plays these roles week after week in the listener's contemporary context.

Second, preaching as an eschatological event is political. It participates in and serves the politics of God—what God is doing "to make and to keep human life human in the world."[7] In other words, eschatological preaching is closely related to God's enterprise of humanization, that is, to "live by faith" as creatures of God, redeemed sinners or believers.[8] It brings into existence what was not there before. Through preaching, the listeners see the world in a new way and aspire to live a life apart from sin, now under the grace of God. They no longer support the politics of the established order or the world's standards of secular ideologies. Those who experience visionary preaching are called to participate in God's politics for the transformation of the world.

In this manner, eschatological preaching is concerned with building the identity of the community of faith. It helps the listeners develop Christian character, vision, and ethos, and provides guidelines or direction for the maturity of the community. At this point, preaching is not a static but a dynamic movement toward the transfiguration of the world.[9]

Last, eschatological preaching is rhetorically persuasive. Its goal is to persuade the listeners to act here and now on the basis of a vision of eschatological hope. It calls the listeners to live as living parables of God's action, so that by their activity people may understand what God is doing in the world and discern God's gracious action toward them.[10] Those who are invited to the parabolic life have the image of God restored in themselves and take responsibility for transforming this world into the realm of God. Their action "signifies the new age that has been inaugurated by Christ."[11]

THE PRESENT SITUATION OF KOREAN AMERICAN PREACHING

How, then, do Korean American preachers understand preaching? What are the characteristics of contemporary Korean American preaching? To understand the present situation of Korean American preaching, I examined recently published sermon books written by Korean American preachers.[12] Although all the sermons I examined did not fall into the same category with regard to theological content and homiletical style, and differed from one another in degree or detail, the majority of them shared four characteristics.

1. *An emphasis on a personal relationship with God.* According to the majority of sermons, Christian redemption means the salvation of the soul gained by born-again faith. They encourage the listeners to accept Jesus Christ as their personal Savior and to increase their faith through devoting themselves to Bible reading, prayer, and church activities. Texts are often used not in their fullness but are subordinated to the personalistic gospel. Some sermons have emotive power to appeal to the individual listener's heart and mind.

For example, Tae-Ho Ahn's sermon based on John 21:1–14 encourages individual souls to surrender their personal problems to God and live with faith in Jesus Christ as follows:

> Do you think that you are alone when you had hard time in your life? The Lord never lets you be alone. When you are distressed, lonely, anxious, and exhausted, Jesus Christ always visits you and asks with concern, "Children, you have no fish, have you?" (John 21:5). He comes to you asking, "Do you bear any fruit of your toil? Do you have joy in your life? Is your daily labor meaningful?"[13]

Considering that most Korean immigrants are lonely and tired both physically and psychologically in this foreign land, this individual approach emphasizing a personal relationship with God seems to appeal to the listeners. However, this personal and psychological approach runs both a theological and a sociopolitical risk. That is, most sermons that concentrate on the personal relationship with God are in danger of leading the listeners to ignore the sociopolitical roots of their problems without critical reflection. They often tranquilize the listeners' consciousness by giving them temporary relief rather than offering the liberating message of the gospel to challenge them to solve their problems.

2. *An emphasis on God's blessing as the fruit of personal devotion and faithful commitment to church activities.* It is not an overstatement to say that more than 90 percent of the sermons I have examined are about how to obtain God's blessing. God's blessing is perceived as personal and material rewards in this world. Contrary to the Scriptures, as Jung Young Lee indicates, most sermons do not understand "joy, peace, goodness, and love"

as God's blessings; rather, they convince the listeners that spiritual blessings are manifested in such worldly benefits in this life as wealth, health, longevity, psychological comfort, and prolific childbearing.[14]

Korean American preachers emphasize in their sermons that God is the only source of these worldly blessings and that such blessings are given to individuals according to the degree of their personal piety and commitment to the church. Likewise, the blessing of God is understood to be conditional. One sermon describes this ideology of blessing thus:

> [Fifteen] years ago, I was an associate pastor in the Oriental Mission Church (in L.A.). One family immigrated to the U.S. with three children. They worked so hard that they could become the owner of two gas stations and buy a nice house in a suburban area. In the beginning of their immigrant life, they devoted themselves to the church. They came to the church every Sunday and kept it holy. However, when they were stabilized economically, they preferred playing golf and going fishing to going to church. One day, the father went fishing on a Sunday and fell down out of hypertension. Although he was moved to the hospital, he passed away. . . . The way of blessing is to obey God with awe . . . the key to blessing is in God's hand.[15]

The key to gain these blessings is to live according to the Word of God; to live according to the Word of God is to participate actively in church services and programs.

The ideology of the present-centered worldly blessing long existed among Koreans through an indigenous Korean religion, shamanism, even before Christianity was introduced to Korea. Koreans believed that the most blessed in the world were those who obtained five blessings from heaven — wealth, success, health, longevity, and many children at home. Korean Christians understood the Christian gospel from their indigenous religious perspective and easily identified the blessing of God with the shamanistic conception of blessing. They believed that the major goal of becoming a churchgoer was to gain these blessings from God, who was the real source of the blessings.

Among Korean immigrants, this ideology of blessing was confirmed by the prevailing idea of the American Dream, which is popularly recognized as "the right to private property, material comfort, and the family."[16] In fact, most Korean immigrants identify with the American Dream on an individual level because the major motivation for their immigration to the

United States was the desire for personal economic prosperity and higher education for the children.

Korean American preaching has catered to this prevailing secular idea of the American Dream by emphasizing the listeners' personal devotion to the numerical growth of the church as the key to accomplishing the American Dream. It has neither awakened the listeners from the illusion of the distorted individualistic American Dream nor corrected the misconception of the blessing of God. Rather, Korean American preachers have narrowed their theological views to a present-centered, individualistic materialism, and have ignored the future-oriented communal and holistic aspects of the blessing of God. As a result, they separate the Christian gospel from the socioeconomic, political, and cultural context of the listeners.

3. *An emphasis on faith that leads to positive results.* Many Korean American preachers understand the Christian faith to be the key to gaining positive results. This understanding can be seen clearly in their illustrations.

Illustrations play a major role in most Korean American sermons. A large number of them are anecdotes, episodes, and biographies of successful persons that demonstrate positive results of their faith. The preachers convince the listeners that such stories can be their stories. Preaching based on these illustrations seems to appeal to Korean immigrants because it encourages them to have dreams for a successful future and gives them confidence in coping with present hardships.

For example, Hyo-Sup Choi's *The Joy of Love* is a treasury of illustrations. He quotes many positive stories from biographies, newspapers, journals, novels, and poetry, and tries to give courage to the listeners through them. His typical illustration is like this:

> There is a modern miraculous story. It is about Harold Walters who was a TV actor. He was sentenced to death because of cancer. When he was offered by Bloomington Christian movie company in Illinois state to act as Christ in the Passion narrative, he decided to play preparing himself to die on the stage. However, when he recited, "Father, I finished my mission. I commend my spirit into your hands," he felt heat in his body and recovered from the cancer. After two years since that miracle, he came back to his career. This is a miraculous story about a person who lives looking high toward the mountains.[17]

Illustrations provide concrete reality for abstract concepts of biblical language and expression. However, when illustrations always focus on various positive experiences of healing and answered prayer on an individual level, they are in danger of distorting the essence of the Christian message because they give the listeners the impression that the gospel itself is a present-centered and success-oriented message, and Christianity is the "religion for winners."

4. *An emphasis on the church-growth model of evangelism.* Korean American preaching stresses mission. Many preachers understand one of the major tasks of the church is mission, and they reflect this thought in their sermons. The sermons reveal that the preachers identify Christian mission with evangelizing the unconverted, recruiting church members, and having their own church buildings. They stress that the listeners should commit themselves to the numerical growth of the membership and instruct them on how to bring newcomers to the church. Some preachers seem to regard the success of the parish ministry as the numerical growth of the church, and their sermons focus on how to increase the members and how to fulfill their plan of having their own church buildings. They convince the listeners that if they commit themselves to the growth of the church, they will be rewarded by God with the material blessing in this world.[18]

Remembering that many Korean American churches rent Euro-American church buildings and that sometimes they have conflicts with the landlord congregations because of the cultural differences between them, it is to some extent understandable that Korean American congregations want to have their own church buildings. In a sermon by Dong-Sun Yim, for example, we can see this. Yim says that his church members have prayed to God for their own church building, fasting forty days in rotation. The preacher convinces the congregation that God will bless the individual members with three things if they achieve the goal of their own church building — material blessings, the blessing of safety, and a blessing in spirit. He concludes the sermon by giving three reasons why they should build their church building: to glorify God's name, to make God happy, and to have their offspring enjoy the blessings in this world.[19]

Korean American preachers limit Christian mission to the evangelization of unbelievers and the numerical growth of the local church. Although this understanding has contributed to the dramatic growth of Korean American churches, their sermons do not help the listeners increase their spirituality or realize their responsibility as Christians for the community to which they belong. They neither give direction for the future of the Korean American church nor offer a vision of a better society for the Korean immigrant community. Instead, they run the risk of creating fierce interchurch competition.

As we have seen in this discussion, Korean American preaching tends to reduce Christian faith and theology to a present-centered individualistic dimension. This tendency is deeply related to the general trends of Korean preaching. The characteristics of Korean preaching have been transplanted and reinforced in the particular context of Korean American churches by Korean pastors who had educational and ministerial backgrounds in Korea. Many ministers in Korean American communities have come from Korea since the 1965 Immigration and Naturalization Act, which granted permanent residency to qualified ethnic ministers. These Korean-trained church leaders have perpetuated a traditional ethnic identity in Korean American communities without self-examination. They have regarded the Korean church as their ministerial model and followed its theology and practice in their preaching, rather than created their own context-specific theological vision.

Korean American preaching needs to become more sensitive to the particular sociopolitical and cultural context of the Korean immigrant community if it hopes to build an eschatological vision for a new world. For this, it is necessary to analyze the present context for their preaching with theological insight.

THE CONTEXT FOR KOREAN AMERICAN PREACHING

Korean American preaching has assumed that U.S. society is as open to Korean immigrants as it is to other Americans for achieving the American Dream. In fact, the reality is different. The Korean immigrant community, like other minority groups, faces fundamental structural discrimination based on race. Racism has been connected with the political, socioeconomic, cultural, and moral dimensions of society. It has caused injustice in every aspect of the Korean immigrant community. There are three particular areas of injustice.

1. *Anti-Korean prejudice and hate crimes.* The average U.S. citizen has little knowledge of the history and culture of Asian Americans, beyond their representation in print and electronic media. However, the media have portrayed Asian Americans with bias. According to a report of the U.S. Commission on Civil Rights, until the early 1970s, the mainstream media in the United States depicted Asian Americans largely as citizens of Asian nations rather than naturalized U.S. citizens, and often in connection with wars such as World War II, the Korean War, and the Vietnam War. As the economies of Japan, Korea, and other Asian countries have

become increasingly competitive with the U.S. economy, the media have begun to regard Asians as economic competitors. On the basis of this prejudiced propaganda, many U.S. citizens insist that Korean and other Asian immigrants "steal" jobs from them.[20]

Likewise, Korean immigrants have often been portrayed in a negative light. The cultural ignorance of reporters and editors of major newspapers and magazines often misinterprets Korean cultural, social, and political matters. They refer to "the inferiority of people of color" and thereby perpetuate ideological justification for Euro-American superiority.[21]

This biased portrayal by the media has encouraged anti-Korean prejudice and discrimination, resulting in numerous hate crimes against the Korean immigrant community. The Los Angeles riots of 1992 revealed that Koreans were caught in the middle, blamed or scapegoated for the economic frustrations of African Americans. In addition, numerous hate crimes against the Korean immigrant community have been committed, reported or unreported. According to Andrew Sung Park,

> In August 1993 a man shot a Korean-American grocer in Washington, D.C., took a potato chip package, and walked out slowly. It was surmised that the motive was not robbery but racial hatred. In the same month someone broke into a Korean-American house at Rowland Heights, California, and left a burned swastika and racially insulting graffiti on a rug and a wall inside. About the same time, a New York policeman hurled racial epithets at a young Korean-American woman and then hit her. Her "crime" was a parking violation.[22]

Despite the inclusive ideal of American society reflected in Korean American preaching, which states that everyone, regardless of color, is rewarded for working hard, the reality is that the Korean immigrant lives in a hostile and racist environment. What is worse, Korean immigrants are politically powerless. There is no political coalition or leading group to advocate for the Korean immigrant community against such unjust treatment.[23]

Most crimes against Koreans stem from the Americans' lack of knowledge about Korean history and culture. These Americans have little understanding of Korean immigrant history and the roots and context in which rich and complex histories, values, thoughts, and feelings exist. Instead, they perceive Asian Americans as a single stereotypical group of foreigners.

Korean Americans have often been viewed as a "model minority." Applying this stereotype to Korean Americans has created yet another problem, leading Americans to ignore the very real problems that Korean Americans face as immigrants, such as language problems, unfamiliarity with the American way of life, and the lack of a solid socioeconomic base in the United States.[24]

This racist context challenges Korean American preaching to expand its boundaries into the sociopolitical realm and to deal with unjust problems arising from racism. Korean American preaching can no longer rest on the individual level focusing on a personal relationship with God, stressing the salvation of the individual soul and born-again faith, or on the local church level emphasizing its numerical growth.

It is important for Korean American preachers to analyze racism within the community and address it for several reasons. First, there is a need to awaken the listeners to their realistic problems. Second, preachers need to provide listeners with comfort that neither tranquilizes their consciousness against injustices nor promises an easy resolution for them. Last, sermons need to offer a hope based on God's eschatological promise that God will overcome the evil power of the world and restore the sovereignty of Christ Jesus. This is a hope that encourages the listeners to take action to transform the community, through positive interactions and corporate relationships with other ethnic groups by which they can better understand others and take reciprocal responsibility for unity and harmony in society. Therefore, Korean American preaching is responsible for building an inclusive society in which everyone understands that all humans are created sacred in the image of God.

2. *Unequal distribution of wealth and classism.* As we have seen in Korean American preaching, Korean American preachers are apt to describe the United States as God's promised land flowing with milk and honey. They often stress economic success as the American Dream's proof of accomplishment, and suggest positive thinking and faith as the means of making the dream come true. They say that if the listeners are diligent and faithful to God, they will be blessed and succeed economically. This concept of positive thinking is commendable. However, the reality is different. Although most Korean immigrants struggle hard, the average population is included among the lower or lower-middle class in income. They work hard just to stay in place, leading to increased stress and workplace injuries.

This problem is fundamentally grounded in an unjust economic system in the United States. Mergers have enabled many larger corporations to preserve profits, thereby establishing monopoly capitalism. In this compressed economic situation, most Korean immigrants are shut out of the mainstream because of a language barrier and the racist and exclusionary nature of the industries that supply better jobs. Despite their higher education, they are unable to find jobs. These people are, in a sense, surplus labor, accepting jobs at a very low wage for service employment or surviving in sweatshops.[25] For those who operate retail or small businesses, surviving in a competitive economic condition is hard. They often compete with other minorities, and when the competition becomes fierce, racial tensions flare. On the other hand, for those who have professional jobs, surviving in the racist economic condition is hard. They soon run into the "glass ceiling" in employment, leaving them discouraged and left out of society, and feeling like failures.[26]

Monopoly capitalism has also contributed to the unequal distribution of wealth. According to an Internal Revenue Service report, in 1989, 1 percent of the population controlled 37 percent of the wealth (up from 31 percent in 1983). Furthermore, 10 percent of the population controlled 86 percent of the wealth. In 1993, 15.1 percent were below the official government poverty level. According to a 1994 report, 10 percent of the total population was hungry or depended on soup kitchens or food stamps.[27] At this point, Doug Henwood criticizes North America for having "the smallest middle class and the highest poverty rates in the First World."[28]

While the unequal distribution of wealth widens the gap between rich and poor and fosters economic recession, political campaigns have exploited poor immigrants, making them the target for this economic recession and slow economic growth. They tend to paint all immigrants as welfare beneficiaries and brainwash the majority with a negative image of new immigrants.

Such structural problems in the U.S. economic system challenge Korean American preachers to ponder the concept of "economic democracy"[29] and consider a different set of values to establish the kind of society we will have and to fight against the abuses of the system from the perspective of the Christian gospel. This vision for the reign of God relativizes our present economic system, where the gap between rich and poor is great, and gives a clue for the development of a new model in which those who have been hired late "for his vineyard" will earn "the usual daily wage" equal to that of all others (Matt. 20:1–16).

Therefore, Korean American preachers who acknowledge the unjust economic system within the community cannot repeat the traditional message of the blessing of God based on the individualistic moralistic conception of reward and punishment. Instead, they need to understand that individual blessing cannot be gained unless the U.S. economic system and structure are transformed for the communal well-being. As long as an unequal system and unjust structure prevail in the American economy, there is no hope for economic prosperity within new immigrant communities. Their preaching must inspire a new vision for the Korean American community and stimulate the listeners to cooperate to make that vision come true within the community.

3. *Cultural imperialism and identity crisis.* For Korean immigrants, the prerequisite for becoming American has been to leave their culture at the door. Korean immigrants, young and old, educated and ignorant, poor and rich, have to go through "resocialization," a process of value change, role redefinition, and the learning of new and modified role behaviors and a new self-image. Their home country values and morals run head-on into U.S. values and morals. Differences in habits, customs, and language make them feel psychologically restricted and imprisoned in the U.S. social context. They often lose or confuse values and the meaning of life.

This resocialization process requires Korean immigrants to expend enormous energy and perseverance, at the same time feeling conflict, anxiety, dissatisfaction, and frustration. This is due to two problems. On the one hand, U.S. public services cannot help new immigrants sufficiently to settle into their new land. Many Korean immigrants arrive in the United States with little background about American society. They need professional bilingual/bicultural counseling services to help them in their personal, social, and academic development. Such services, however, are not available for most Korean immigrants. For example, quality court interpreters are not available to facilitate understanding for Korean immigrants who are not fluent in English. In addition, cultural barriers discourage them from using the courts. Asian Americans make up only 0.7 percent of the lawyers nationwide, although they constitute 2.9 percent of the U.S. population.[30] In the context of public education, a lack of services for new immigrants' children in the public schools increases the chance of dropout among Korean high schoolers. According to statistics, language-minority dropout rates are twice as high as those for nonlanguage-minority students.[31]

On the other hand, the process of resocialization forces immigrants to be Eurocentric. Public school education focuses on a Euro-American way of life, giving great weight to European history, culture, and language. It does not include sufficient knowledge or appreciation of Asian values, history, or culture. This curriculum fosters a cultural gap and, with the undermining of immigrant self-esteem, contributes to conflicts between immigrant parents and children.

This public educational system, which has served cultural imperialism, should definitely be reformed in view of society's pluralistic and multicultural trends. In other words, mainstream teachers must learn about immigrant students' cultural backgrounds and their needs, and educational curricula should have balance in order to hold the interest of all students. They should include Asian history, language, and culture so that they can provide all Americans with informed knowledge about Asian Americans and can help Asian Americans understand their roots and have pride in them. Such an effort would promote inclusiveness of American culture and enhance intercultural relationships in American society.

Cultural imperialism in American society creates an identity crisis among Korean immigrants. The question of "Who am I?" is intensely problematic at a certain stage of an immigrant's life. The lack of life satisfaction (psychological) and job satisfaction (socioeconomic achievement) increases this identity crisis. When immigrants feel that the dominant group will never fully accept them and that the United States is not a "melting pot" society for them, they experience marginality, and their marginal situation creates anxiety, confusion, and insecurity.[32]

Faced with this identity crisis, first-generation Korean immigrants tend to have a double identity. They regard themselves as Koreans who are temporarily sojourning in the strange new land of the United States. They consider the possibility of going back to their homeland of Korea rather than staying in the United States permanently. Such double status discourages them from taking any reciprocal responsibility for American society as Korean American citizens, and leads them to be unconcerned about any interaction with other ethnic groups. It deprives them of an opportunity to extend themselves into mainstream America and encourages them to be introverted as traditional Koreans, preserving patriarchal and authoritarian hierarchism within the immigrant community.

Second-generation Korean Americans, who were born in the United States and have already accepted the dominant American culture as a norm for their lives, experience an identity crisis more profoundly than that of the first generation. They feel themselves neither Korean nor American. While they resist the implanted hierarchical traditional values of Koreanness within the Korean immigrant community, they confront rejection by the mainstream American culture because of their racial and cultural difference. No matter how well they might be assimilated into American culture, they are treated as Koreans or foreigners by other Americans. In this predicament, they constantly struggle to give meaning and labels to their self-identity.

In this context, one of the most urgent tasks of Korean American preaching is to help the listeners build an identity as Korean Americans. Their identity means Korean immigrants are "both Koreans and Americans at the same time." As Lee describes, Korean immigrants have rich spiritual, religious, and cultural resources from their heritage and are expected to create the best synthesis possible in the American cultural soil.[33] This understanding of ethnic identity should be applied not only to Korean immigrants and other minority groups, but also to white majority people in this multiracial American society.

The understanding of the Korean American identity as both Korean and American rather than either Korean or American is grounded in a vision for American society from the biblical perspective of the eschatological community, in which all members are equally respected by one another as the children of God and live harmoniously side by side. Korean American preaching based on this vision will contribute to the formation of Korean immigrants' identity by means of new images and stories created from the reinterpretation of Korean culture and tradition in light of liberating words of God.

DECONSTRUCTIVE AND CONSTRUCTIVE THEOLOGICAL TASKS

The evaluation of the present situation of Korean American preaching and the analysis of the context for preaching reveal that contemporary Korean American preaching has not sufficiently responded to the realistic problems within the community. Although it has been playing a major role in influencing the Korean immigrant community, Korean American preaching has not addressed the issues of justice for the community with the prophetic voice. It has spiritualized and moralized the listeners' everyday suffering from social injustice, without helping them to challenge society to improve itself with the liberating words of God. If Korean American preaching shrinks the liberating message of the Christian gospel to materialistic and individualistic size, encouraging the listeners to endure and stay in their place, there will be no future for the community.

At this juncture, Korean American preachers are called upon to sing a radically new song in this strange new land of the United States. Singing a new song is possible only when Korean American preaching is transformed into an eschatological event that creates a new vision for the future of the community from the perspective of God's saving story. The practice of singing a new song needs homiletical renewal through a twofold theological task based on the nature and function of eschatological preaching. It must, on the one hand, deconstruct the dominant ideologies in society and, on the other hand, construct a new vision for communal well-being.

1. *The deconstructive theological task.* Korean American preaching as an eschatological event confronts the established order or the world's standards because God's eschatological power is revolutionary, opposing the structural, sinful power of the world. It does not support the distorted images of the American Dream grounded in present-centered individualism, materialism, exclusive ethnocentrism, and sectarianism, but recognizes them as illusions or false hopes.

Eschatological preaching views individuals as integral parts of society and reflects their personal faith and relationship with God in the context of the community to which they belong. It no longer focuses on messages of the individual successes of the listeners or the numerical growth of a local church. It realizes these are not enough for fulfilling the eschatological vision for the community. Instead, it helps the listeners to recognize their suffering and hardship not merely in relation to personal faith but also to the structural sociocultural problems inherent in the community. It challenges them to struggle against these injustices.

In this regard, Korean American preaching as an eschatological event has an obligation to deconstruct the dominant injustice in society and the distorted image of the American Dream within the Korean immigrant community. The process of deconstruction works like this: First, the preacher questions the established value system and symbolized worldview on behalf of the oppressed community. Second, the preacher evaluates these with critical insight from the perspective of God's eschatological power to transform the world. Last, the preacher dismantles the dominant prejudice and injustice, and names them sins before God and others.

If Korean American preaching ignores this deconstructive task and is silent on these profound and acute sins, its silence means that the Korean American church sanctions injustice within the community.

2. *The constructive theological task.* Korean American preaching as an eschatological event must not only deconstruct the distorted images of the dominant ideologies but must also construct an authentic vision of a new world. It does this by creating a vision for the community. It provides direction for that community by opening the listeners to a future-oriented hope. The future hope is not part of any present sequence but is a radically different new world in Jesus Christ because the eschatological power of Christ overturns the dominant ideologies and promotes equality and justice in society.

The eschatological vision for the Korean immigrant community is holistic and communal. It is holistic in that it includes the whole human world — sociopolitical, economic, cultural, and ecological. It describes how human beings live harmoniously as creatures of God in the world. It is communal in that it promotes harmony and unity among different ethnic groups, through sharing their common problems, questions, and goals. It visualizes the communal goal of humanity that includes often ignored minority groups such as African Americans, Latinos, and Native Americans. This eschatological vision is not only a dream but a dream to be realized. It is the constant ideal or imagination toward which we are directed but which we never fully attain.

How, then, can the eschatological preacher construct a vision for the community? God's eschatological vision cannot be described uniformly in all situations but accommodates itself to diverse situations with varying capacity. Thus, the business of vision making acquires a concrete and contextual character according to the particular situation of the community.

For the contextual approach to an eschatological vision, the preacher first listens intently to the Korean immigrants' existential experiences in their concrete everyday lives. The listeners are understood to be "individuals, family units, and social groups."[34] Second, through careful and critical examination with the help of such interdisciplinary studies as politics, sociology, economics, anthropology, and psychology, the preacher sees the listeners' problems from a holistic perspective and discerns what injustices relate to their personal and communal experiences in the context of the community to which they belong. Last, the preacher describes the will of God for the community by discovering how God is at work for their humanization by means of a contextual interpretation of the biblical text.

Here, the Bible has the authority not as an absolute norm for Christian identity, transcending ideology and historical particularity and deriving its authority from such intrinsic properties as literal inerrancy or verbal inspiration, but contextually and functionally as a parable or metaphor. That is, the biblical story goes beyond its literal and cultural boundaries and creates a new meaning in the particular context of the congregation, and functions as the clue that enables the listeners to have access to a new way of looking at the world. When preachers are open to the imaginative power of metaphorical language and images in the biblical text, they can create a new meaning that can guide, nurture, and reform the listeners' lives.[35]

The new vision created contextually for the Korean immigrant community includes a new image and a sense of possibilities through which marginalized minorities can break out of dehumanizing confinement and move toward the liberating possibilities for the future. In this vision, Korean Americans and other minority groups live as true citizens of America.

They contribute to "making America a free, just nation of immigrants and former immigrants," by fully participating in this pluralistic society.[36]

This eschatological vision has power to effect a turning point in the course of U.S. history for the creation of a new world. It can transform the listeners' mode of thinking into a realization that Americans, not only minority but also majority, are marginal people who live in this multicultural society. As Lee points out, each margin of each ethnic group is "the locus—a focal point, a new and creative core—where two (or multiple) worlds emerge."[37] All Americans bring their ethnicities to the whole as components of this pluralistic society and participate in creating a harmony of difference. Likewise, in this vision, the dominant ideologies of Eurocentricity and white supremacy, which are the roots of racism, become inclusive and open-ended, and this new vision inspires "the creation of a beautiful mosaic of colorful people in this nation."[38]

SINGING A NEW SONG IN THE STRANGE NEW LAND OF AMERICA

In this regard, the Korean American preacher is both a dreamer, who dreams of a radically new world as an alternative for the Korean immigrant community, and a politician, who anticipates the realization of this eschatological vision within the community. Through preaching, the preacher reveals the vision and persuades the listeners to participate in actualizing it within the community.

This eschatological preaching has the persuasive power to transform the listeners' mode of thinking and to enact itself anew in their lives by means of a rhetoric of persuasion. The rhetoric of persuasion does not use prescriptive and imperative language, but instead employs the indicative and descriptive moods. It calls the listeners' attention to a narrative that tells of God's saving acts in human history and of God's promise for the human future. Thus, the tone of preaching is not "This is what you had better do, or else!" On the contrary, the tone is rather, "Seeing who you are, where you are, and what you are, this is the way ahead, the way of being and living in the truth, the way of freedom!"[39] It rhetorically invites the listeners to this eschatological vision and promise of God. Through persuasive rhetoric, the listeners extend their view of Christian faith from personal to communal, see the events of their lives in the social, national, and global dimensions, and are called to participate in the divine politics of God.[40]

Therefore, singing a new song in this strange new land of America evokes new hope for the reign of God as a common future for all Americans, majority and minority alike.

CHAPTER SEVEN

A Jewish Perspective

PURSUING JUSTICE THROUGH KNOWLEDGE OF SELF AND OTHERS

STACY OFFNER

I N JEWISH LIFE, there is a tradition of praying a prayer *before* one prays. The Rebbe of Tsanz was asked by a Chasid: What does the Rabbi do before praying? I pray, was the reply, that I may be able to pray properly.[1] In similar fashion, when someone stands before a congregational community, it is critical to pray before preaching. The prayer that I am drawn to pray says a great deal about my understanding of preaching and the role that I believe preaching has in my rabbinate.

I imagine myself about to preach, in my synagogue, standing on the *bimah* just moments before the sermon is to be delivered. My back is turned to my congregation as I am facing the *aron hakodesh*, "the holy ark" that houses the Torah scrolls. I look into that ark, and then up above, and I see the big engraved set of Hebrew letters set atop the ark. The letters are imposing, not so much for their size but for their message. They say: *Da Lifney Mi Atta Omed*, "Know Before Whom You Stand." Those words go through me and challenge me like a prayer. It is my obligation, as a preacher, to know before whom I stand. The words most obviously point to God as the one before whom I stand. But I believe that the power of the words is that they force me to focus as well upon my congregation.

Da Lifney Mi Atta Omed, "Know Before Whom You Stand." How dare I preach to people whom I do not know? The words require me to think of my congregants—each of them as an individual, and all of them together as a unique community of people—before I write a sermon and before I deliver a sermon. Before I begin to craft any message, I picture their faces and invoke their presence. I must think of who they are, what their circumstances are, what their troubles might be, what they are knowledgeable about, what their needs are. It is my obligation to know them in order to preach to them. My own rabbi of blessed memory, Rabbi Jacob Rudin, encouraged me with his words: "If you do not love those to whom you preach, you will not preach successfully. If, secretly, you do not respect those who listen to you, then you will not touch them deeply."[2] To preach effectively, a preacher must engage in serious reflection upon the lives of the individuals who sit in the congregation, in order to come to know them, to love them, and to respect them.

What is the purpose of preaching? What is the goal? I know there are many answers to this question. I can hear my chaplain friends saying that the goal of a sermon is to heal. I can hear my educator friends saying that the goal of a sermon is to teach. Other rabbis say that the goal of a sermon must be to draw people to cleave more closely to our people Israel. Other voices within me come up with other worthy goals. A sermon is to inspire. A sermon is to touch deeply. A sermon is to motivate. A sermon is to invite reflection. A sermon is to challenge. A sermon is to probe.

I resist the temptation to place any of these purposes in a hierarchy of virtues. Each is important; each is worthy. Some sermons do all of these things, some do only one, but collectively, many sermons over time serve all of these purposes. I hesitate to offer one single answer to the question regarding a sermon's purpose because a sermon by its very nature must be holistic. Our spiritual core is not reached by compartmentalizing; so too, a preacher must resist the temptation to focus rigidly on one goal at the expense of any other.

Of course, the best way to be holistic in our task is to bring the whole self to it. And that is no easy challenge. That is, perhaps, the ultimate challenge for the preacher. *Da Lifney Mi Atta Omed*, "Know Before Whom You Stand," has an implied corollary. For to know the One before whom you stand, you must know yourself as well. And that is why acute consciousness of our own social context, our own values and virtues, our own strengths and weaknesses, is critical to our task as preachers. And each time we preach a sermon we must know our own selves in preparation for the task, and we must share our own selves in the process of the task. And that involves risk. For every time we share a bit of who we are with others, we take a risk. Ultimately, then, we might say that the purpose of preaching is to take a risk.

We do many different things in the world that can fall into the category of "taking risks." A man takes up skydiving, and that's a risk; a woman chooses to give birth to a child, and risks are involved there too. Though the ventures may vary, all risk-taking activities have something in common: we have no control over the outcome. Ultimately, the risk that we take as preachers is to bring all of who we are to the task. It sounds so simple, but it is so simple to avoid. As soon as we try to be "preachers" instead of ourselves, as soon as we hide behind our ritual garb, instead of standing in it, we cease to be preachers in the true sense of the word, which means quite literally "to declare in public," and we become preachers in its most pejorative meaning, "givers of advice in a most tiresome manner."[3]

The magnitude of the risk of sharing all of oneself is demonstrated in one of our most powerful biblical stories. The story is about God and Moses and their interaction at the burning bush, but first, a little background. It is important to know that according to Jewish tradition, names are very significant. The name we give to someone says something about that person and even directs the person's path to an extent. So when we name someone *Baruch*, which means "blessed," we actually help to ensure that the person's life will indeed be blessed. When we name someone *Chaim*, which means "life," we help to ensure that the person's life will be full of life. When Moses and God engage in dialogue at the burning bush, Moses asks God what God's name is. God's answer sounds very strange because it does not sound like a name at all, but a declaration. God says to Moses: *Ehyeh asher Ehyeh* ("I am who I am," which can also be translated, "I will be who I will be"). Our challenge as preachers, as in life, is to be who we are. So here we are. Striving to be ourselves. Nothing more. And most important, nothing less.

To be who we are most fully and most honestly, we need to acknowledge what makes us who we are. How do you answer the question: "Who are you?" It is no small task. Indeed, it is not only the things I choose to tell you about myself that reveal who I am to you, but the kinds of things I choose to tell you. We reveal something about ourselves when we choose to describe ourselves by sharing a bit about personality (e.g., whether we are outgoing or shy), physical size (whether we are large or small), gender, the make-up of our families of origin, sexuality, nationality, faith community, ethnic community, or economic status, to give just a few examples. Permit me to tell you some things about myself that I think have particular impact upon how I come to preaching.

HONORING WHO I AM IN HOW I PREACH

I grew up in a predominantly Jewish and predominantly affluent suburb of Manhattan. During my elementary school years, I was not consciously aware that my neighborhood was comprised almost totally of Jews. I was unaware of the fact that my parents and their generation had grown up in far more impoverished circumstances as children of immigrants in Brooklyn and the Lower East Side. Only in my adult years have I recognized the miracle of their journey from a childhood that was steeped in poverty and anti-Semitic playground brawls to an adulthood imbued with economic and professional success. Their life journey powerfully echoed the formative journey of the Jewish people, a journey reenacted every spring during the holiday of Passover, the journey of our people that took place more than three thousand years ago, a journey from slavery to freedom, from degradation to dignity.

From my child's eye view, much more important than the message of Passover was the fact that I had a mother who was always there for me when I came in the door from school; a mom who played board games with me when I was sick, who made me practice the piano, and who made me finish my homework when I didn't want to.

I know that in many respects my childhood was a childhood of privilege. I consider it to have been a privilege indeed to have grown up in a safe, loving home. I know, too, that the fact of that privilege causes me to preach in certain ways, and I need to be ever vigilant to the fact that there are those in my congregation whose childhood experiences lead them to hear different messages from the ones I might intend. For example, a text about homecoming might resonate beautifully to me personally, but what is the impact of a sermon about the importance of returning home on a congregant whose home was not a haven but a hell?

But I am not naive about the successes of my parents' generation. For they also grew up during years that saw the most horrific oppression and persecution ever waged against the Jewish people. Though they lived safely in the United States, it was only an ocean that spared them while radio reports told of the destruction of their extended families under the cruel regime of Hitler's Germany.

I am, at one and the same time, a child of an American success story and a child of the Holocaust generation. Both realities are critically important to who I am and how I preach. Some more important words about who I am. I am a Jew. I am so because I was born of Jewish parents, both of whom were the children of immigrants. My mother's parents came to this country from Poland in the 1920s. I have heard stories of how my grandfather, penniless, left his wife and one child in Warsaw and played cards in stowage on the boat to the United States, where he was coming to escape persecution and find a new and better home for his family. He had been a furrier in

Poland, settled on New York's Lower East Side, went into the garment business, sent for his family and, by the time my mother was born, had taken up residence in nearby Brooklyn. My father's parents had lived in the countryside of what was then the Austro-Hungarian Empire and also came to this country in the hopes of finding the American Dream. My father, like my mother, was born in Brooklyn.

My parents were the American-born children of Yiddish speakers who wanted very desperately to enter into the stream of American life and culture known in their day as the great American melting pot. Their parents had been Orthodox/secular Jews; my parents were more strictly secular Jews, though when they moved out to the suburbs of Long Island, they joined a synagogue to give their children a Jewish education. I am, therefore, a third-generation American Jew, raised in a secular household that maintained membership in the local Reform synagogue. The secularity of my upbringing still has a strong hold on me, even as I probe notions of God, faith, and matters of the spirit. The fervor with which my parents and their generation pursued the American Dream was not lost upon me. I do not take my American citizenship for granted, and I add that to the many privileges that are mine.

I am reminded of an exercise that I frequently use with my confirmation class of tenth graders. I ask them all to stand in the middle of a room and point to the four corners of the room, each of which is marked with a sheet of butcher paper. The four signs say: AMERICAN, MALE, FEMALE, and JEW. I ask them to walk to the corner of the room displaying the sign that best describes them.

Whichever they tend to choose, it is always an evocative exercise. Through the years, I have become aware less of the choice they make and more of the power of their commitment once they make a choice, even though they all acknowledge struggle and difficulty in making a choice.

In some ways, the choice is an artificial one, for we can be all the things that we claim to be. Especially in the United States of today, we can choose the communities that we desire to affiliate with, and we are free to affiliate with as many as we choose. Nevertheless, I also believe that the exercise leads us to clarify for ourselves which community or identity we choose to make primary. Of course, this whole notion of "choice" is so very American, and so very antithetical to Judaism. In keeping with America's emphasis on the individual, it is not difficult at all to see ourselves as primarily individuals, who pick and choose communities in which to belong. But Judaism believes that the community itself is primary, and out of the context of community we develop as individuals.

It is therefore very clear what the answer to the exercise is for me. Though I am an American, a Jew, and a female, the identity that resonates most strongly and most profoundly is that of being a Jew. The reasons are manifold. Being a Jew is itself many things. I do not have to choose between my culture and my faith and my people because being Jewish is at once being part of a people, a religion, an ethnic group, a culture, and a civilization. The very fact that Judaism is simultaneously a religion and an ethnic identity has caused me to struggle to express myself in the context of this book.

Let me explain. The title of this book is *Preaching Justice: Ethnic and Cultural Perspectives*. Each author of each chapter represents a different ethnicity and/or culture. But what the others have in common is the faith of Christianity. My situation is different. I am the only person representing a non-Christian faith, and I am the only person whose ethnicity and faith are one and the same. Because I am a Jew, it is not the voice of my ethnicity and my culture that I bring to the principles and practices of Judaism; the experiences of ethnicity and culture that the Jewish people have in common have given voice and shape to Judaism itself.

It is no accident that throughout the Hebrew Scriptures, the Jewish people are not called "believers in Judaism," for there was no "thing" called Judaism. Rather, they are called "the children of Israel," for familial identity is primary. The beliefs of that family were yet to unfold, and unfold they did out of their ethnic and cultural experience. For example, our primary theological story, the move from slavery to freedom at the time of the Exodus from Egypt, is a theological story rooted in the historical experience of the Jewish people. We *were* slaves in Egypt. That real experience of culture and peoplehood shapes the theological thrust of Judaism.

Cynthia Ozick has lamented that when she stands in the midst of a gathering of women, she is defined as a Jew; when she stands in the midst of a gathering of Jews, she is defined as a woman:

> In the world at large I call myself, and am called, a Jew. But when, on the Sabbath, I sit among women in my traditional shul and the rabbi speaks the word "Jew," I can be sure that he is not referring to me. For him, "Jew" means "male Jew." My own synagogue is the only place in the world where I, a middle-aged adult, am defined exclusively by my being the female child of my parents. My own synagogue is the only place in the world where I am not named Jew.[4]

Ultimately, the fact of my being a woman and the fact of my being a Jew are inseparable. I am both simultaneously. Sometimes the experience of being both is in conflict and is a source of great pain. Often the experience of being both is in harmony and is a source of great joy. It has been said that in many respects, the experience of being Jewish actually parallels the experience of being a woman.[5] Women value relationship more than individualism, the expression of emotion more than stoicism, and women know the experience of being oppressed by those with greater physical strength. These, too, are the values and experiences of being Jewish; being both Jewish and female only accentuates their importance and their role in shaping a compelling notion of justice that permeates every preaching moment.

I believe that a sermon is always interactive. Sometimes the interaction is more obvious than other times, but a sermon is always interactive. I sometimes use a manuscript when preaching, I sometimes use an outline, and I often engage my congregation in ways that give them the opportunity to answer questions and express themselves verbally within the context of the sermon. This methodology is extremely effective, and it is largely so because of the makeup of my particular congregation.

I am the rabbi of a small synagogue founded in 1988. At the time of our founding our membership consisted of 40 households. We have grown since then to more than 280 households. The purpose of our founding is still very much a part of the synagogue today. In the words of the congregation's Mission Statement:

> We are coming together as a community to provide a place of Jewish worship, learning and assembly. Our focus is the building of a caring inclusive community in the spirit of liberal Judaism. We welcome individuals and families of varying Jewish lifestyles. We are particularly sensitive to the need for inclusion of both traditional and non-traditional family structures, and for the development of an appropriately inclusive ritual life that enriches our Jewish experience. We recognize that study of Torah is an on-going life-long process. We hope to encourage and support one another as we grow in our studies and apply the wisdom and principles of our heritage in acts of loving kindness and social responsibility.[6]

True to its mission, the reality is that my congregation is filled with people of varying Jewish lifestyles. At any given time, the sanctuary will be filled with single adults, married people, gay and lesbian people, young children, teenagers, interfaith couples, mixed racial families, and traditional families. One of my goals as a preacher is to speak to all of these people in such a way that each feels addressed and respected.

Let me illustrate with an example, for the task is far more easily articulated than it is accomplished. On one Shabbat evening before Chanukah, I planned to speak about Chanukah and the message of economic justice that it brings. I learned earlier in the week that we would be having some guests at our service, about fifty older citizens from the Jewish Community Center. As I thought about the composition of my congregation that evening, I knew that there would be "strangers" (guests) mixed in with friends. I knew, too, that my congregation was by and large very young, and that these guests would be particularly noticeable because they were older. I wanted to honor them, engage them, and need them, that is, I wanted to need their expertise in some way, which I believe is one of the highest forms of respect. I wanted to do this all right away so that my sermon could continue with everyone convinced that I was speaking to all.

My message was one of economic justice. Central to my message was the economic truth that a dollar cannot be spent in two places at the same time. I likened it to the adage that a person cannot be in two places at one time. And then I knew how I would invite these older citizens to be a necessary part of our community. There is a Yiddish saying regarding the impossibility of being two places at once. I am not a Yiddish expert, and so I relied on the older citizens present to come up with the phrase. The sermon manuscript I prepared began like this:

My sermon tonight is about Chanukah and, more specifically, about Chanukah and its message of economic justice and economic reform. But first, I have a question to ask, that I am eager to ask, given the special makeup of our congregation this evening.

What I would like to know—just raise your hand right where you are—is, How many of you this evening can speak Yiddish? Great! Then you might be able to help me out. There's a Yiddish proverb I've been thinking about, and I don't remember how it goes. It's about how if God wanted us to be in two places at one time, we would have been created differently. You know that one? (*Get it from a congregant.*) Thank you! That's the one. I've been thinking about that proverb all week, in relation to this: (*Hold up dollar bill.*)[7]

By asking the question I was able to engage the older citizens, recognize their presence, affirm their reality, and demonstrate an appreciation of the unique wisdom they bring rather than just say a perfunctory, "How nice it is to have you here with us this evening."

One other evening I was giving a sermon about preparing for Passover. Because Passover is a holiday that takes place in the home, I wanted to be sensitive to the fact that we cannot take for granted that everyone has a home in which to celebrate. So too, also because it is a home-based holiday, I know that Passover is celebrated in a variety of ways, and I wanted to honor that. And so I wrote:

> I am sure that the preparations for Passover are as different and varied as the people in this sanctuary. Each of us prepares for the holiday in a unique and personal way, even as we are guided in our preparations by the wisdom, teaching, and traditions of our people.
>
> One person's preparation begins weeks, perhaps even months, before the holiday itself as invitations are extended to friends and family members who live both near and far away. Hosting the Seder means thinking about guest lists, preparing grocery lists, counting the chairs, and counting the Haggadahs. Hosting the Seder involves a huge set of responsibilities, but it also relieves one of the anxiety of not knowing whose Seder he or she may be invited to this year.
>
> Of course no one should be without a Seder to attend. The adage "There's always room for one more" becomes an obligation at Passover time. That is why Shir Tikvah has its own Seder, so each one of us is assured a place at the Seder.
>
> Whether we are hosting a Seder or attending Seders as guests, or doing a little of both, everyone has to prepare for Passover because Seder or no Seder, Passover comes to all Jewish homes.[8]

Preaching to the same congregation every week for almost a decade makes me keenly aware of the many variables that go into the preaching moment. No two moments are alike, and the success of any sermon is often unpredictable. When a sermon works, it is because rabbi and congregation are present to one another in the moment. All sorts of factors combine to make this possible or impossible, including the liturgy, the music, the weather, the seating arrangement, the world events of the week past, and, yes, the sermon manuscript.[9]

A TIME TO TEAR DOWN AND A TIME TO BUILD

In recent years, the Jewish community has been increasingly willing to examine the ways in which it treats its own vulnerable people. If indeed our history and our theology combine to suggest that we are a people who know firsthand the horrors of oppression, and therefore we are a people committed to loosening the shackles of oppression for all peoples, then surely we are obligated to look scrupulously at our own behavior and point the finger of challenge at ourselves when justice requires it. Nowhere has there been more examination of and challenge to some of Judaism's traditional rubrics in the past twenty years than in the realm of the status of women.

I would cite three examples of basic injustices toward women within Judaism that pervasively reinforce women's exclusion from equity in Jewish life. I choose these three examples because they come from three significant arenas, the biblical, the liturgical, and the *halachic*[10] literature.

Biblically, there is probably no more famous example of women's exclusion than the verse cited in the book of Exodus at just the moment when the Jewish people are to receive the Torah. Imagine being a woman, sitting in the synagogue, listening to the reading of the Torah, and being captivated by the drama of the Jewish people preparing to receive God's Torah. At the very moment that will solidify the covenant between God and the Jewish people, Moses instructs: "Prepare for the third day; do not go near a woman" (Exod. 19:15).[11]

The power of that rejection and that exclusion caused Judith Plaskow, a leading Jewish feminist theologian, to title her book about Judaism from a feminist perspective *Standing Again at Sinai*. The very title of her book suggests that we must not reject the covenantal story, but we must claim it for ourselves by standing there again. Though I believe very strongly that the biblical text as handed down to us is not to be altered, so do I believe very strongly that it is the preacher's challenge (and opportunity) to *stand again at Sinai* every Shabbat morning.

Our ability to stand there again is rooted not only in a modern sensibility about justice, but also in an ancient theological conviction about Sinai. The Jewish teachings regarding Sinai have long held that all Jews— those living, those dead, and those yet to live—were/are present at Sinai. The very concept gives the women and men of today the invitation, the opportunity, the obligation, to have been present at Sinai. The contemporary scholar Leonard Fein muses over the notion of Sinai:

> Now, the question of whether or not there was a Revelation at Sinai seems
> to me considerably less important than the question of whether or not I
> was there. The first question requires of me a faith I do not have, cannot
> invent, and regard (perhaps for that reason) as irrelevant; the second re-
> quires of me a faithfulness that is mine to offer. . . .

"Were you there?" . . . is an invitation as much as a question. "Were you there?" means, among other things, "Do you choose to associate yourself with the event/story/idea? Do you accept what it implies, whether or not you accept that it actually happened?" It is plain (to me) that when I say, "I was there," I am not speaking an empirical truth; I am offering my consent. I am freely choosing to associate myself with a myth I find uplifting, informative.[12]

Sinai implies a relationship, a holy relationship, that binds the community of Jews together with God through mutual responsibilities and obligations. It is the preacher's responsibility to make sure that all know they are invited, "from woodchopper to waterdrawer," to use the language of Deuteronomy 29:10, and also to add the language of current times, from male to female, from able-bodied to disabled, from those who are married to those who are single, from those who are gay to those who are straight.

Surely, the most famous prayer of exclusion in the liturgical literature is the prayer in the morning blessings of the traditional siddur that states: *Baruch Atta Adonai, Eloheynu Melech Ha'olam, Sh'lo Asani Isha* ("Blessed are you Adonai our God, Ruler of the world, who has not made me a woman"). This blessing comes in the context of a triplet of blessings that stem from a Talmudic dictum: "Rabbi Meir used to say: Every man is obliged to recite three blessings each day: Who has made me an Israelite . . . Who did not make me a woman . . . Who did not make me a slave."[13]

An aside: I want to say at this moment that we have already wrestled with this one. We have already done this work. When I say "we," I mean, generally speaking, the progressive, feminist Jews of North America. Much of the reaction to texts like this can be found in books published ten and twenty years ago.[14] I can assure you as well that the prayer books of liberal Judaism have eliminated the prayer that offensively negates women, and have changed the wording of the line regarding slaves into the more positive "Who has made me to be free." So, task accomplished, why do I lift up the problem here once again?

I do so because of the dictates and realities of justice. Freedom is never won just once. Justice must be protected again and again and again. That is why, in some respects, I am grateful that we are forced to examine the words of Torah anew each and every day. How easy it would be to "edit out" offensive language. We can do it in our sermons, we can do it in our liturgy, but we cannot do it in our Torah and we cannot do it from our history. We are forced to confront injustice all the time.

I also lift up the offending texts because of the requirements of honesty. We cannot be honest about who we are if we refuse to be honest about who we have been. As Rachel Biale, a noted scholar of Jewish legal literature, explains:

> In order to engage in meaningful Jewish discourse today, and to formulate personal and communal ways of "being Jewish" in the modern period, it is necessary to acquire a shared "Jewish language," which is the language of the traditional Jewish sources. If we master the language of these sources and use them as an anchor, we can talk about contemporary problems in a way that connects them to what is already known and crystallized. Other- wise we sever the connection with the past on which our world rests. In order to understand what puzzles and concerns us in the present we must turn to the past, even though it may at first be more confusing, obscure, and alien than our present. In the case of Halakhah, for many Jews today, and for Jewish women in particular, learning the language of the past is learning a foreign language. Yet this language is crucial, not only in order to understand the history of the Halakhah and what Jewish life has been, but also to formulate Jewish life and aspirations today.[15]

The prayer thanking God "for not making me a woman" is not so easily expunged because this liturgical injustice is actually based on a halachic injustice. In other words, the prayer that offends is a reflection of a prin- ciple embedded in the halachic/legal texts of Judaism. Though the prayer no longer appears in the prayer books of liberal Judaism, it continues to appear in the traditional/Orthodox prayer books, which base its inclusion on halachic grounds. The traditional explanation of the manifestly offen- sive prayer is that this is *not* an offensive prayer; rather, it is based on men's thankfulness for receiving the obligation of so many mitzvoth. Had they been women they would not have this opportunity for service to God: "The Tosefta explicitly gives the reason for the berachah [blessing] concerning woman as her not being obliged to perform as many mitzvot as man."[16]

Of course, this explanation begs the question as to why women are not obligated to perform mitzvoth as are men. The traditional response to this is further apologetics:

> A few later authorities have taken the fact of women's exemption from various commandments as evidence of the greater ease with which women achieve spiritual goals. The Maharal of Prague (d. 1609) views the ex-

emption as reflective of the nature of woman's personality, which is naturally closer to the serenity necessary for spiritual achievement. He writes
that the performance of mitzvot and the learning of Torah are designed
to enable human beings to achieve spiritual perfection. Man's aggres-
sion is a detriment to his spiritual aspirations and he therefore must work
harder and be given extra religious tasks. Women, however, because of
their greater potential for spiritual growth, require fewer mitzvot to achieve
spiritual perfection. Thus, he says, the Talmud tells us that the reward
promised to woman is greater than that promised to man. It is assumed
that they will generally achieve higher levels than men.[17]

Why is this "compliment" so unsatisfactory? Beware the justifications
for exclusion that are made by those not so excluded. Jews of all genders
should be particularly sensitive to the calls for exclusion of women, for we
as a people have long been excluded by those more powerful than ourselves.

The horrors of persecution and vilification are etched deeply into the
Jewish psyche. We have experienced these abuses in every age, but never
so dramatically as during the Holocaust. The lessons of the Holocaust have
had a vast impact on Jewish theology and the Jewish pursuit of justice in
these post-Holocaust years.

Of the many ramifications of the Holocaust, I would cite three phenom-
ena that come to my mind as enduring.

1. *No longer can we ever take our safety for granted.* Even now in the
United States, where the Jewish community enjoys unparalleled success,
we who are its members are burdened by the possibilities of history and
challenged to fulfill the admonition: "Never again." An excellent example
of the way this experience of injustice maintains its impact is revealed in
this reverie of Rabbi Harold Kushner:

> A group of us were sitting over coffee and cake in one family's living
> room. We were all Jewish, members of the congregation I was then serv-
> ing, and we all had young children. In the midst of the conversation
> about local and national politics, one of the wives asked, "If a Nazi-style
> government were to come to power in the United States, how many of us
> know a Christian family we would trust to hide our children?" What I
> remember about that conversation is not that some of us had close Chris-
> tian friends and others didn't, but that *nobody in that room thought it was
> a ridiculous question.* Nobody expected it to happen, but nobody consid-
> ered the possibility unimaginable.[18]

In the midst of apparent success in this country, the possibility of persecution is ever present.

2. *To the extent that any one people or population is not free, we all are at risk.* The Jewish pursuit of justice is both beneficent and self-serving. The Holocaust was about the Nazi attempt to annihilate the Jews and to destroy millions of other people as well. Martin Niemoeller's words speak powerfully to the Jewish psyche:

> First they came for the Communists
> and I did not speak out—
> because I was not a Communist.
>
> Then they came for the Socialists
> and I did not speak out—
> because I was not a Socialist.
>
> Then they came for the trade unionists
> and I did not speak out—
> because I was not a trade unionist.
> Then they came for the Jews
> and I did not speak out—
> because I was not a Jew.
>
> Then they came for me
> and there was no one left
> to speak out for me.[19]

To seek justice for others is not only a mitzvah, it is not only inherently right; it is in the most practical of terms expedient.

3. *In the face of extermination, our mere dedication to our survival is an act of justice.* Jews have long argued whether a focus on our community's survival is an act worthy of direct attention. Survival for its own sake, the argument goes, is hardly a worthy goal. But after the Holocaust, self-survival has indeed come to be understood as a worthy goal, so much so that Emil Fackenheim, the noted Holocaust theologian, has boldly suggested that we adopt a 614th commandment: "The authentic Jew of today is forbidden to hand Hitler yet another posthumous victory."[20]

From the crematoria of Auschwitz, where to find faith once again? An old theological story of the creation of the world provides just such a healing understanding of the meaning of our lives. Judaism has a beautiful faith story that has come down to us from the kabbalah, the teachings of Jewish mysticism. The mystics tell us that when God created the world, God took some fresh new light and poured it into vessels to send out into the world. The light was too powerful for the vessels, and the vessels shattered. What should have been perfect, what should have been whole and proud and beautiful, found itself broken and in need of repair. And so from the very moment of creation, the task of every human being has been *tikun olam*, the repair of the world, the picking up of the pieces and putting them back together again.

The story of *tikun olam* has been embraced by twentieth-century Jews who understand Judaism to be fundamentally of this world and who see in the story a call to perform acts of social justice. I get great pleasure from the fact that the story of *tikun olam* is a rallying cry for the social action movement within Judaism, and that it originated with the mystics. The story of *tikun olam* fuses social action and mysticism and reminds us that spirituality and social action are, in their essence, one and the same. Repairing the broken places and people in our world has everything to do with the life of the spirit. The task of the preacher is to tend to the life of the spirit. It is therefore, ipso facto, a call to preach justice.

THE IMAGE OF JUSTICE

I believe that the preaching of justice must be a part of *every* sermon. To fully understand how to make justice a part of every sermon, it is important to understand the Jewish perspective on the concept of justice. One of the most well-known texts that teach us about justice is the biblical verse in Deuteronomy that says: "Justice, justice shall you pursue" (18:20). This one sentence alone teaches us much about justice. Let us look for a moment, word by word, at this verse. The first word, "justice," is a translation of the Hebrew word *tzedek*. The Hebrew word is most often assumed to mean "justice," but it is alternatively translated as "righteousness," "virtue," and "equity." All four of these translations of the word *tzedek* are reflected in the verse "Justice, justice shall you pursue," which, as the commentary suggests, is nothing less than a "distillation of the Torah's prescription for the social ordering of society. No people gave as much loving attention to the overriding importance of law equitably administered and enforced as did Israel."[21]

The repetition of the word "justice" is a reflection of just how critical the pursuit of justice is. One commentator has suggested that "the double emphasis means justice under any circumstance, whether to your profit or loss, whether in word or action, whether to Jew or non-Jew. It also means do not use unjust means to secure justice."[22]

And the words "shall you pursue" remind us that justice is not assumed to be a perfectly achievable state of being, but a goal to which we aspire. We must be constantly engaged in the pursuit of justice, even though a perfect state of pure justice is impossible to achieve. The inability to achieve perfect justice is never to be used as an excuse to forgo the pursuit of justice.

I am intrigued by the notion that "equity" is a synonym for "justice." Indeed, Everett Fox, in his recent translation of the Bible,[23] chooses to translate Deuteronomy 18:20 this way: "Equity, equity, shall you pursue." It may very well be that justice is found in the pursuit of equity for all. What does equity mean in this diverse country of ours? I should not think that "equity" means "equality," for to honor difference is to make distinctions. To treat everyone equally is to ignore diversity. But to treat everyone equitably is to ensure a qualitative fairness of our behavior.

A fundamental component of being Jewish in this country (or in any country outside Israel) is being part of a minority. Jews represent about 2 percent of the population of the United States and about 1 percent of the population of Minnesota. Much of the pastoral work that I do with members of my congregation, from the children to the adults, is related to the experience of being a part of a minority. In Religious School, many of the children use the opportunity to talk about what it is like to be the only Jewish student in their secular school classes. It is both a privilege and a burden. Adults also struggle to navigate through a dominant culture not their own. Being a part of a minority is not inherently just or unjust, but given the challenges of assuring equity for all, the potential for injustice is ever present and must be guarded against vigilantly.

If justice, in large measure, means equitable treatment, then the converse is also true: injustice is about being treated inequitably. The most profound image of inequitable treatment is that of the slave; the most unjust institution created by human beings is the institution of slavery. It is not a coincidence that the story of the Jewish people begins with the story of our enslavement. The command to pursue justice that appears in Deuteronomy is rooted in the experience of a people whose slavery is described in the book of Exodus. The motivation to follow the command of Deuteronomy is rooted in the experience of Exodus.

As it is written in Exodus 22:20, "You shall not wrong a stranger or oppress him, for you were strangers in the land of Egypt." The pursuit of justice is rooted in our experience of injustice. Also in Leviticus 19:34: "The stranger who resides with you shall be to you as one of your citizens; you shall love that one as yourself, for you were strangers in the land of Egypt." The message is repeated time and again throughout the Torah, and culminates in this message in Deuteronomy 23:8: "You shall not abhor an Egyptian, for you were a stranger in the Egyptian's land." It is an article of faith that out of the experience of being oppressed comes the foundation for a life dedicated to not oppressing others. Not only shall you not oppress others, but as Deuteronomy 23:8 points out, you shall not even oppress those who oppressed you.

In striving for justice for all, how is justice most effectively pursued and most effectively protected? The Jewish community in the United States has answered that question in a number of ways. As a minority committed to the pursuit of justice, we have worked vigorously to safeguard the protections granted in the Bill of Rights: "We have always deeply believed that the Jewish community—indeed any minority—exists and flourishes best in a society that is informed by social and economic justice, and especially by the principles and protections that inhere in the Bill of Rights, particularly the First Amendment and most centrally the separation of church and state."[24]

Being a part of a minority people means that we are obligated to pursue justice for ourselves. Being a part of a minority people means that we are obligated to pursue justice for all minorities. And being a part of a minority people means that we must be ever vigilant to pursue justice for others within our own minority people.

And so we come to Judaism's most important prayer, its most important proclamation, its most important challenge:

Sh'ma Yisrael, Adonai Eloheinu, Adonai Echad.
Hear O Israel, Adonai Is Our God, Adonai Is One.

A proclamation of monotheism to be sure, but also a command to unity, and a command to listen. If God is one, then we are *all* God's children. We must *hear* that message. We are commanded to listen. Justice requires listening. The irony, of course, is that a preacher's task is to speak. But more important, a preacher must listen. *Da Lifney Mi Atta Omed,* "know before whom you stand." Listen to those before whom you stand. Hear the experience, the pain, the injustice, the joys, the needs, the longings, of those before whom you stand. Only then is it time to give voice.

You will know you are ready to give voice when you have imagined every circumstance and every scenario about which you choose to speak, from the vantage point of the other. You will know you are ready to give voice when the voices of those who cannot speak are heard in your voice. You will know you are ready to give voice when you have prayed that you might preach. You will know you are ready to give voice when you have taken to heart the admonition to *Da Lifney Mi Atta Omed*, to "know before whom you stand." Only then will your voice be a preacher's voice. And the preacher's voice will be a voice of justice.

CHAPTER EIGHT

A Lesbian Perspective

MOVING TOWARD A PROMISED PLACE

CHRISTINE MARIE SMITH

PREACHING AS A CRAFT and act of ministry brings together several worlds: the world of texts, the world of religious traditions, the world of a community's psychological and spiritual needs, and the world of the larger social context in which people live. Because it is first and foremost a theological act, preaching is a ministry of public theological naming. Yet preaching is more than an act of naming and interpreting past and present reality; it is also a constructive theological act. It gives shape to, and actually creates, personal, social, and ecclesiastical reality.

White Western male Christian preaching often has taken the biblical text and the tradition as the primary starting points for preaching. For many preachers of social, economic, and cultural privilege, unquestioned and ultimate authority is still given to Scripture and tradition in the preaching act. This homiletical focus is in real contrast to the particular witness of preaching that emerges within communities of oppression.

In the craft of preaching there have been too many generalizations, universal claims, and assumed truths put forth from voices of power and privilege. With contemporary social and theological awareness, we know that such generalizations and claims perpetuate domination and oppression at the expense of human specificity and diversity. Preachers must begin to claim the truth that all preaching is done within very particular social and religious communities, and it is thoroughly influenced by the social location of the individual preacher.[1]

SOCIAL LOCATION: MY LESBIAN EXPERIENCE

I knew from the time I was quite young that I was different. From the middle of my adolescent years I have known that I am a lesbian. The early years were years of absolute silence, isolation, and terror. I first came out to my parents and sister in my early twenties. After that, a few close friends in my early seminary years kept expanding my circle of confidants ever so slightly until my mid-twenties when I discovered the larger lesbian community in Columbus, Ohio. This discovery changed my life. It broke into my personal and social isolation, broadened my sense of community, and immersed me in the politics of lesbian/feminist thought. In this initial discovery of the lesbian community, the "closet" door swung open in a way I had not known was possible. For the last twenty years, it has been a slow, steady process of keeping the door open. Sometimes it has closed tightly again, only now to have it flung open in ways I cannot yet fully comprehend or understand as preacher, teacher, and scholar of the church.

Given the reality of closets for lesbian and gay people, I have been trying to find my voice, my truth, my community, and much of my life. I have spent most of these years afraid: afraid of hurting my family, afraid of losing friends and colleagues, afraid of being attacked, afraid of being fired, and afraid of losing my ordination. I have been afraid, afraid I dress, walk, talk, and move in the world in ways that keep me from ever being really acceptable as a woman. I have spent a lifetime intentionally not wearing baseball caps, sneaking into the men's department to buy shirts and jeans, sitting on fishing piers all night with groups of strangers (almost always all men), feeling often that I'm not quite sure if I'm dressed okay, making myself try to carry a purse, laughing and making light when my nephew or niece hears someone call me sir. It isn't just the fear that keeps me from my voice, my truth, my life; it is the constant heavy sense that I am alien, strange, marginal. In the past few years I no longer have feared losing job and ordination, but even as I move my life into more and more public arenas as an out lesbian, anxiety, fear, and strangeness persist.

I have been preaching for more than twenty years, and I have written about and analyzed the oppression of heterosexism and homophobia and its implications for the ministry of preaching. This is the first time, however, that I have sought to articulate some of the very particular ways my lesbian identity—and the larger lesbian and gay community—profoundly influences and informs my theological analysis, my homiletical practices, my preaching voice. I am able to write from within this identity because of the historical legacy, the present collective support, and the transformational vision of the larger gay, lesbian, bisexual, and transgender community. My voice resides within that community and emerges out of it, and for this I owe a profound debt of gratitude.

Perhaps the context to which I am most indebted is my own congregation, Spirit of the Lakes United Church of Christ, in Minneapolis. It was birthed in 1988 as a church that would particularly serve and respond to the lesbian, gay, bisexual, and transgender community. It is one of the few congregations in the country within mainline Christianity where gay and lesbian people are the majority of the congregation. In this context I have been fortunate to have a supportive and challenging place to discover some aspects of my lesbian preaching voice and to observe many other gay and lesbian preachers.

SOCIAL LOCATION: NAMING ONE'S COMMUNITY

Even though the community of which I am a part is spoken about often as the gay, lesbian, bisexual, and transgender community, I am choosing to focus my reflections primarily on lesbian and gay voices. It is not my intention to exclude bisexual and transgendered voices, but to focus upon and honor some of the distinctive lived experiences and understandings of gay and lesbian people within the church that give rise to a ministry of preaching justice. This choice will be both criticized and celebrated, and indicates in a profound way the complexity of our struggle for justice and liberation.

Risking simplicity, I want to explore a bit further some of the ways lesbian and gay people understand our lives and the social and ecclesiastical changes that are needed. These are by no means definitive statements, but are descriptions of some of the complex philosophies and strategies that give shape to the whole lesbian and gay liberation movement. These philosophies and strategies will directly influence one's understanding of preaching justice.

Some gay and lesbian people want to be integrated into mainstream culture and the church with all the rights, privileges, and acknowledgments that accompany heterosexual relationships. I would describe this arm of the movement as a movement for personal and social equal rights. Persons who voice this position do not necessarily raise a serious critique of the fundamental nature of our social, political, and ecclesiastical reality, nor would they necessarily see what affects the lives of lesbian and gay people as systemic oppression. Preaching from this perspective might involve focusing on the sacred quality of each human being's life and the justice of all people being treated with equality.

Some gay and lesbian people are forging a movement toward greater relational freedom and sexual choice. I would describe this arm of the movement as a movement toward sexual liberation. Persons who voice this position also do not necessarily raise a serious critique of systemic and social structures; rather, the primary issue is freedom of expression in every area of our relational and sexual lives. Preaching from this perspective might involve forging a positive, sacramental understanding of human embodiment, sexuality, and relationality, and the justice of all people's sexual and relational expressions being acknowledged, respected, and treated as incarnational goodness.

Some lesbian and gay people want to create and shape new understandings of relational life, gender identity (gender fullness or gender independence, rather than gender complementarity), sexuality, community, covenant relationships, theology, and spirituality. I would describe this arm of the movement as a movement toward radical social and ecclesiastical transformation. For these gay and lesbian people, equal rights, assimilation, and even celebrated sexuality will never be enough. Ours is a much more radical critique of basic gender identity, male-female role constructions, heterosexist social systems, culture, and theology. Sexism and heterosexism are seen as social systemic expressions and structures of oppression to be resisted and transformed. This understanding stands in real contrast to what I believe is the more limited vision of equal rights and sexual freedom. Preaching from this perspective might involve naming and indicting the many and varied oppressive faces of heterosexist privilege and domination, and proclaiming the vision of a world free from restrictive and violating gender constraints and idolatrous sexualities. This is where I would locate my analysis and work.

To understand the different dimensions or arms of the movement for change among lesbians and gay men is crucial, and to understand the kinds of analyses that shape and inform these different positions is equally important. All of these positions and the differences they reflect are embodied in the real lives of religious lesbians and gay men. All of these differences are present in our churches and within the congregations in which we preach. Lesbian and gay preachers, and preachers who choose to be in solidarity with lesbian and gay people, will need to struggle with these differences. They compel us to honestly discern our assumptions and convictions about lesbian and gay liberation, and they urge us to become more aware and articulate about how these differences shape and influence our common life. The complexity of the movement for change challenges us as preachers to name and incarnate every conceivable redemptive expression of saving work among us.

ECCLESIASTICAL INJUSTICE:
A COMPELLING AGENDA FOR PREACHING

Gay and lesbian people experience a multitude of individual, social, and political injustices. A primary expression of that injustice is ecclesiastical oppression and violence, which will be the focus for most of the following reflections.

There are so few places in the religious life of this country, and in the Christian church in particular, where the transformational quality of lesbian and gay lives can be talked about and celebrated. There are so few places where we can move beyond the church's minimal acceptance of lesbian and gay people; beyond how to interpret Scripture so that the humanity of gay and lesbian people remains intact; beyond how to theologize in ways that justify the ordination of lesbian and gay ministers; beyond conversations about how to reduce our lives in every conceivable way so that no one in the church feels threatened. For many lesbian and gay people the church has been our greatest source of fear. At times it has offered us community, life and hope, grace and resurrection, yet often at enormous costs.

A heavy, smothering blanket of silence and condemnation has been laid across most of our familial, social, and religious lives. That smothering blanket exists in our homes, in our workplaces, in our backyards, in schools, in public parks, on sandy beaches, and in almost all our churches. It is everywhere. We have moments of reprieve from it—marching in pride marches, walking the streets of Key West or Provincetown, entering the doors of some of the churches we attend, sitting in front of a fireplace in our own homes—but all of us know it is only a reprieve.

The smothering blanket of silence is always there. We must cast it off so that we can breathe, think, walk, and love; so that we can construct and create new theological thinking, and reflect creatively on the religious meaning of our lives. Oppression oftentimes has so fundamentally silenced us that not only do we have a difficult time naming and articulating our reality, but we are forced to spend our life energy trying to remove the blanket and to assimilate into realities that are not our own. No preacher can know or touch the lived realities of lesbian and gay people without first acknowledging and responding to this smothering blanket of silence.

Often lesbian and gay people experience the church as a primary agent of this repressive violence, promising life and hope on the one hand, yet ultimately silencing us on the other. Mitsuye Yamada, a Japanese American woman, in a poem entitled "Playing Cards with the Jailer," invites us into the strange, paradoxical reality of colonized, oppressed lives:

> A brief metallic sound
> jars
> the quiet night air
> hangs
> in my ears.
> I am playing cards with the jailer
> who shifts his ample body in his chair
> while I fix my smile on his cards
> waiting
> My eyes unfocused on the floor
> behind him where a set of keys spiderlike
> begins to creep slowly across the room.
> Come on come on your play I say
> To distract him I tap the table
> Wait.
> With a wide gesture
> he picks up the keys
> hangs them back on the hook
> Yawns.
> The inmates will keep trying will keep trying
> Their collective minds pull the keys
> only halfway across the room each time
> The world comes awake in the morning to a stupor
> My brown calloused hands guard two queens and an ace
> My polished pink nails shine in the almost light
> I have been playing cards with jailers
> for too many years.[2]

Growing numbers of lesbian and gay people understand fully that almost every category of religion, faith, theology, and life has been defined and proclaimed as universal truth by "jailers": jailers of economic power, jailers of privilege and imperialism, jailers of heterosexism, jailers of ecclesiastical authority. For gay and lesbian people to become prophetic theological voices, we have to stop waiting to be freed, and we must discern carefully all the ways we continue to "play cards with the jailer." For too many of us that jailer is the church. Many of us love the church passionately, yet we are discovering that to stop playing cards with the jailer is an act of survival and resistance.

THEOLOGICAL INSIGHTS AND TASKS

A significant and profound dimension of oppressed people's theologizing is that it takes place within, and comes forth from, community. As diverse and sometimes divided as the lesbian and gay community is, I believe that we experience our lives as being part of an oppressed people. Oppressed people share the experience of oppression, the experience of struggling for survival, the experience of individual and collective resistance to oppression, and the experience of community as a central locus of hope. Out of some of these shared experiences, certain religious and theological concerns and themes emerge from within the lived experiences of lesbian and gay people.

SURVIVAL AND RESISTANCE

One of the first theological assertions that lesbian and gay people are making with their very lives is that survival and resistance are powerful expressions of religious vocation, ethical agency, and profound faithfulness. Carter Heyward, a lesbian Episcopal priest, speaks about this resistance ministry as what is shaking the foundations of the church: "If we are to live with our feet on the ground, in touch with reality, we must help one another accept the fact that we who are christian are heirs to a body-despising, woman-fearing, sexually repressive religious tradition. If we are to continue as members of the church, we must challenge and transform it at the root."[3]

Lesbian women and gay men are challenging the church to dismantle much of this kind of theology. The voices that are preaching justice from within my community are urging us to stop denying the rising number of teenage suicides among gay and lesbian young people;[4] they are asking us to probe the theological and religious dimensions of "coming out," the violent distortions of selective biblical hermeneutics, and the powerful connections between relational sexual power and God's redemptive activity.

To really understand the quality and character of lesbian and gay lives, you must understand the deep religious and theological significance of struggle, survival, and resistance. The survival and resistance of gay and lesbian people involve redemptive, saving practices, resurrection moments, and hope-filled communal relationships. Our individual and collective religious task is not just "embracing the exile,"[5] as John Fortunato helped us to understand, but empowering the resistance community of gay and lesbian people to lead the church into new life.

CHRISTO-PRAXIS

Oppressed people who are trying to theologize out of their lived experience are involved in a very important Christological movement within the Christian church. Many voices are describing this movement as a movement from "Christology" to "Christo-praxis," a movement away from an exclusive and primary conversation about Jesus of Nazareth and Jesus as the Christ and the relationship between these two aspects of our faith, to a focus on what it means in our religious lives to embody and incarnate redemptive, saving activity: "In this praxis theological knowing would cease to be a matter of discovering *the* Christ and would become instead a matter of generating together images of what is redemptive or liberating in particular situations."[6]

The second Christological assertion emerging from within the lives of lesbian and gay people has to do with salvific activity that enables people to cast off blankets of smothering silence, and activity that empowers people to stop playing cards with jailers. When gay and lesbian people are empowered by the church to liberate ourselves from the power and authority of oppressive jailers of all kinds, the whole religious community participates in redemptive, saving activity. When we refuse to relinquish the church to hatred and oppression, when churches and synagogues provide true sanctuary and vital religious meaning in the lives of lesbian and gay people, these communities become sites of resistance and places of redemption.

Some churches and preachers are involved in complex and varied forms of Christo-praxis in efforts to move toward communities of justice regarding lesbian and gay lives. Some of our communities simply believe that the church needs to become a welcoming home for gay and lesbian people. Their Christo-praxis involves responding to the concrete pastoral and religious needs of gay and lesbian people. Preachers who see their work within this category may, for example:

1. Speak to the very real issues of lesbian and gay families.
2. Draw upon the stories of lesbian and gay long-term relationships to teach our congregations about fidelity and commitment.
3. In dialogue with lesbian and gay members, probe the particular spiritual and theological issues that are distinct and central to their lives.
4. Develop a critical awareness and suspicion about the stifling absence of lesbian and gay voices within Scripture.

Some of our churches focus attention on the nature and reality of *homophobia* (a profound fear of people who are lesbian and gay). Their Christo-praxis tries to analyze the nature of this fear, its origins and its manifestations, and attempts to shape and create ways to resist and transform it. Preachers who see their work within this category may, for example:

1. Challenge members of the congregation to more deeply understand and to dismantle the homophobic fears present in their attitudes and actions.
2. Help members of the congregation make fundamental connections between homophobia and all other fears that produce violence and oppression.
3. Enable people to see homophobia as a pervasive social reality rather than simply an individual and private fear.
4. Utilize stories, poetry, movie scenes, and songs to draw people into moments of possible conscientization and conversion.

Some churches may be ready and able to reflect upon and explore more fully the impact of traditional Christian theology on the lives of gay and lesbian people. This Christo-praxis work involves deconstructive, critical theological and ethical reflection (that is, critiquing the destructive and oppressive theologies within Christianity that have oppressed and silenced lesbian and gay people), and it involves the constructive work of theologizing out of the distinctive realities of lesbian and gay lives. Preachers who see their work within this category may, for example:

1. Indict the continual use of "texts of terror"[7] within the Bible, used to silence, judge, and condemn lesbian and gay people.
2. Explore biblical texts that portray female-female and male-male relationships that are exemplary for our lives of faith.[8]

3. Examine and analyze how traditional theological concepts and themes have excluded the experience of lesbian and gay people, and what theological themes speak with relevance and depth.
4. Engage in biblical and theological study with members of the congregation who are lesbian and gay with the specific goal of broadening the theological content of one's preaching, and also empowering lesbian and gay members to preach directly their own religious truths.

Some church communities approach the task of Christo-praxis by clearly and boldly focusing their attention and their analysis on heterosexism, the systemic oppression and injustice of the "normative" social structuring of our social reality based exclusively on heterosexual relations. Their work involves a thorough critique of the church's role in justifying and maintaining the exclusive institution of heterosexuality. Preachers who see their work within this category may, for example:

1. Challenge heterosexual people to name, understand, and dismantle all forms of heterosexual privilege.
2. Work to enable the congregation to make clear connections between heterosexism and all other forms of oppression, such as sexism, white racism, classism, ageism, ableism, militarism, and imperialism.[9]
3. Name heterosexuality as a form of social and relational idolatry.
4. Explore and analyze gender beyond the bounds of male-female, dominant-submissive, man-woman dichotomies.

Still others of our communities of faith express the work of Christo-praxis by engaging in strategic, political work, trying to change the attitudes, the polity, the systems of hierarchical and heterosexist power at every level of the church's denominational life. Preachers who see their work within this category may, for example:

1. Feel it is essential to confront denominational policies and structures in a preaching ministry that extends beyond a local setting and across judicatory and national lines.
2. Advocate for the ordination of lesbian and gay ministers, and speak on behalf of lesbian and gay representation at all levels of denominational life.
3. Work to assure the presence of lesbian and gay preachers and voices

in local, national, and international denominational and ecumenical events.

4. Preach in ways that empower an entire congregation to strategize for broader ecclesiastical change.

All of this work is important and needs to be recognized and named as the work of Christo-praxis in our religious communities. It is Christo-praxis work, saving, redemptive work, because it is the ministry of creating welcoming, safe space. It is the ministry of personal and social change on behalf of justice; it is the ministry of deconstructive and constructive theologizing. It is the ministry of resisting oppressive structures that dehumanize and generate violence. It is the ministry of ecclesiastical transformation. The diversity of our expressions of Christo-praxis in the church reflects the diverse understandings of the struggle that exist within the lesbian and gay community itself.

FEAR AND THE HOME PLACE OF SAFETY

I will make with them a covenant of peace and banish wild animals from the land, so that they may live in the wild and sleep in the woods securely. I will make them and the region around my hill a blessing; and I will send down the showers in their season; they shall be showers of blessing. The trees of the field shall yield their fruit, and the earth shall yield its increase. They shall be secure on their soil; and they shall know that I am [God], when I break the bars of their yoke, and save them from the hands of those who enslaved them. They shall no more be plunder for the nations, nor shall the animals of the land devour them; they shall live in safety, and no one shall make them afraid. I will provide for them a splendid vegetation so that they shall no more be consumed with hunger in the land, and no more suffer the insults of the nations. (Ezek. 34:25–29)

This passage from Ezekiel was the primary text for a sermon I preached at United Theological Seminary in 1993 at the convocation Lesbian and Gay Voices Transforming the Church. The sermon title was "A Promised Place." I chose this text, and the title informed by it, because it so powerfully conveys a third essential theological struggle and concern central to lesbian and gay lives. That theological issue centers on the profound sense of fear and existential marginalization that lesbians and gay men constantly experience, on the one hand, and the creation of safe place, home place, promised place, on the other.

CREATING HOME PLACE

Chris Glaser speaks poignantly about what gay men and lesbian women might teach the church about creating homes in the midst of unwelcoming environments and isolating exile:

> I believe that the vision of homemaking keeps many lesbian and gay Christians in ministry within the church and within their community. Christian scholar John Boswell shares that vision. During one of his visits to Los Angeles, he gave a lecture on those periods in church history when homosexuality was tolerated and sometimes celebrated. At a clergy luncheon a minister asked what were some of the special graces gay people had to offer the church. The first grace Boswell mentioned was our ability to treat one another as family. . . . We have created home for one another in the midst of a society and church which treats us as strangers. And that has been one of our saving graces throughout history.[10]

From the moment that they discover who they are, gay and lesbian people must learn how to create experiences of home, salvific places of safety forged in the midst of social and ecclesiastical violence. This reality of having to create home, and never being able to assume the reality of home in one's life, is a truth religious leaders need to understand and grasp, not just with our intellects, but with our hearts and spirits.

A CRITICAL VIEW OF EXILE

Myles Alexander, a gay United Church of Christ minister, in a statement made at Spirit of the Lakes United Church of Christ in Minneapolis, spoke about the concept of *exile* in ways that resonate with questions I am beginning to raise as well about the use of that language to describe our experience. He suggested that "exile implies there is a homeland from which one came and to which one might return. But for lesbian and gay people there is no homeland, there has never been a homeland."[11]

Although I have referred to the concept of exile in my work, I now wonder why so many lesbian and gay people have used that term. A lesbian and gay biblical hermeneutic invites us not simply to appropriate exile as a theological concept that describes our lives, but to find our theological voices in trying to describe the distinctive terrain of our experience of being without a home place.

Joining the "Company of the Despised"

In *Gay Theology Without Apology*, Gary Comstock adds a layer of meaning to this existential angst. Upon walking through the doors of the first gay bar he had ever entered, he comments, "By stepping inside I began to become what I had always feared. With relief, and also with a measure of trembling, I was finding my own salvation—joining the company of the despised and finding sensitive, intelligent, and friendly people to love."[12] It is a strange and somewhat horrible irony that for lesbian and gay people to move into a sense of being at home, to move from isolation to community, we must individually, socially, and publicly join the "company of the despised" with real intentionality. A ministry of preaching justice will empower lesbian and gay people to join their own community, no matter how despised by a heterosexist society and church, in order to find the safety of home.

One impact of "playing cards with the jailer" too long is that so many lesbian and gay people believe the isolation they experience is more the product of their lives than it is the result of systemic oppression. When one chronically feels without a sense of belonging, or a profound sense of home, one begins to believe that something very fundamental and basic about one's humanness must be flawed, distorted, unhealthy, and ultimately shameful. This shame is so pervasive and so strong that it deeply affects many of us even in the midst of wonderfully joy-filled relationships, fine parenting, and strong and creative vocational expressions in the world. Understanding the depth and breadth of this shame and rejection is a major challenge for those of us who will be pastoral, religious, and theological leaders. How does this chronic state of not belonging shape and form a people over time? How will our preaching reflect a deep understanding of this existential reality?

Essex Hemphill, a prophetic African American gay man, expresses it in these painful and poignant words:

> Surely it is one kind of pain that a man reckons with when he *feels* and he *knows* he is not welcome, wanted, or appreciated in his own homeland. But the pain I believe to be most tragic and critical is not the pain of invisibility he suffers in his homeland, but the compounded pain and invisibility he endures in his own home, among family and friends. This occurs when he cannot honestly occupy the spaces of family and friendship because he has adopted—out of insecurity, defense, and fear—the mask of the invisible man.[13]

THE POWER OF GRACE

I continue to try to understand the depth and breadth of grace as an important dimension of faith for our homiletical agendas that might be strong enough to respond to this persistent condition of being rendered invisible and without safe home.

Grace is the freely given divine gift affirming that all people have a rightful place in the universe and a sacred place in the human community. No one deserves or merits God's grace, yet it is given as unconditional and persistent gift. As religious leaders and preachers, we need to understand clearly that even though heterosexism and homophobia keep many of our religious communities from being homes of grace for gay and lesbian people, nothing can prevent the essence of a just and loving God from being the home of grace for all, and nothing can prevent gay and lesbian people from being the home of grace for one another.

SITES OF RESISTANCE

Desiring and seeking a safe home place is just one religious response we might make to the pervasive human experience of marginalization. In her book *Yearning: Race, Gender, and Cultural Politics,* bell hooks gives us an alternative way of conceptualizing this persistent reality and helps us link it to the redemptive, saving power of resistance work:

At times, home is nowhere. At times, one knows only extreme estrangement and alienation. Then home is no longer just one place. It is locations. Home is that place which enables and promotes varied and everchanging perspectives, a place where one discovers new ways of seeing reality, frontiers of difference. . . . For me this space of radical openness is a margin—a profound edge. Locating oneself there is difficult yet necessary. It is not a "safe" place. One is always at risk. One needs a community of resistance.[14]

Whether as lesbian or gay persons we are placed on that margin due to the oppression of others, or whether we are a part of the heterosexual community that chooses to place our lives there in solidarity, hooks is challenging us to interpret this state of marginality and silence as an opportunity to live within a radical openness, and on the edge of risk and danger, in order to construct a different world. She is also inviting us to acknowledge that living in this radical open place forces us to take community seriously, and to engage our lives with communities of resistance. bell hooks believes that marginality is not just a "site of deprivation," but it is a place of radical possibility, a space of resistance.[15]

How might our theologizing change were we to imagine the experiences of marginality more as places of radical openness, radical possibility, and sites of resistance? What would our churches have to do to be true sites of resistance? How might preaching move whole communities closer to this mission?

RESURRECTION

The fourth area of theological meaning that I want to lift up from within the lives of lesbian and gay people is resurrection. Many people in our religious communities speak about resurrection as the dramatic, new life that happens exclusively to individuals after bodily death. However, I believe that Christianity is about forming a people who take seriously resurrection in their everyday lives, and move their bodies and lives into places where their embodied power can make a difference. What would it mean if our preaching called us to place our flesh and blood wherever people hurt and suffer, wherever the innocent are violated and oppressed, wherever people are struggling for life? Wherever embodied love and presence exist with vitality and strength, wherever people refuse to abandon life, or whenever the power of death cannot silence the power of life, I believe we are standing in the presence of resurrection.

Resurrection life is something we are and can be for one another in community. Jack Pantaleo, a gay man who writes about his recovery from being raped by a stranger, speaks vividly about the power of community that enabled him, and can help us, to climb out of the grave: "On the anniversary of the rape, a group of my closest friends held a healing service in my apartment. They laid hands on me to pray away the degradation from that awful night. After the service, one of my friends stayed with me the entire night and held me. . . . My community reached their hands into my tomb of self-hate and doubt and loved me. . . . They untied my grave clothes with the most unrelenting tenderness."[16]

This story speaks about the power of resurrection life to heal degradation and also gives us a very private, yet communal picture of resurrection and its power to "untie our grave clothes." A biblical text often theologized about among lesbian and gay people is the raising of Lazarus (John 11:28–44). We know something distinct about the tomblike quality of closeted existence, and we know something very concretely about the mandate given to those who loved Lazarus, "Unbind him, and let him go."

The grave clothes of heterosexism and homophobia are legion, enough so that all of us could spend a lifetime untying them. And lesbian women and gay men know that untying the grave clothes of closeted living is absolutely impossible without a community of resistance and support. Preaching justice in solidarity with lesbian and gay people will challenge heterosexual people to develop the skill of untying grave clothes.

Resurrection is acts of insurrection. Resurrection is not just the untying of grave clothes in community; it is also something we embody in our radical social and political acts in the world, our acts of insurrection. Robert Goss, in *Jesus Acted Up: A Gay and Lesbian Manifesto*, says, "A gay/lesbian liberation theology begins with resistance and moves to political insurrection. . . . Retrieval of the 'dangerous memories' of Jesus is appropriated into gay/lesbian narratives of resistance. The memories of Jesus' suffering and memories of their own homophobic oppression fuel insurrection."[17] Ecclesial confrontations, expressions of resistance to the church's heterosexist power and control, are redemptive forms of insurrection and saving moments of resurrection power.

Resurrection has everything to do with sacrificing death. From the untied grave clothes to acts of insurrection, resurrection has everything to do with freely entering into death. An additional challenge comes once again from the voice of Jack Pantaleo:

> In the life of Christ, we encounter this ultimate sacrifice. Jesus, as we all know, sacrificed his life. Nailed to a cross and crucified, he gave up his very life, echoing his own words that one can have no greater love than to give up one's life for a friend.
>
> What an extraordinary sacrifice that was! Yet it was *not* the ultimate sacrifice, for if Jesus had stopped there, he would be remembered only as another nice teacher who spoke a lot about love.
>
> Let's face it: death had been done before. Anyone can die. Jesus revolutionized creation because he had the nerve it took not to remain dead. Christ went beyond sacrificing his life. He sacrificed his death. He voluntarily let go of the comfort of death and fought to rise above the grave.
>
> The hardest thing we can do is not to die, but to live, and to live abundantly in joy.[18]

It is not happenstance that a gay man identifies resurrection as a sacrifice of death, voluntarily letting go of the comfort of death and fighting to rise above the grave. How would he talk about the relationship of "coming out," which is indigenous to gay men's and lesbian women's experience, and this image of sacrificing death? Closets are stifling, dishonest, and death producing, yet give some comfort and security to those who reside within them. Maybe one has to sacrifice the death of assimilation, the death of acceptability, the death of hiding, and the death of silence to experience resurrection life, and coming out can sometimes feel like sacrificing death.

Resurrection has to do with the liberation of "coming out." One more aspect of resurrection leads full circle to Lazarus. Julia Penelope and Susan J. Wolfe, in *The Coming Out Stories*, give us an additional image of resurrection as coming out, as sacrificing the death of narrow confines that imprison:

> Hence the words *coming out*, if unexamined, suggest that each of us has merely to come out once through a single self-declaration. We have actually to focus on the *-ing* of the process. In heterosexual hegemony, we are taken for straight wimmin unless we declare ourselves; we must therefore come out by degrees, announcing ourselves over and over again. . . . Like the nautilus, each of us must risk vacating chamber after chamber as it grows too confining for her emerging self, in order to create her own new, larger self.[19]

Perhaps untying grave clothes with unrelenting tenderness, sacrificing death, moving into acts of insurrection, and vacating chamber after chamber are all implicit experiences of the power and possibility of resurrection life. These are some of the distinct images for preaching justice that flow from the real lives of lesbian and gay people.

GENDER IDOLATRY AND INCARNATIONAL POSSIBILITY

Hetero-relations and heterosexism cannot be understood apart from sexism and male domination. Heterosexism is a tool of sexism. In a world of male domination, it is unacceptable for a woman to choose a woman. Domination must be maintained. In a heterosexist society, it is equally unacceptable for a man to choose a man. Domination is maintained only if men fulfill the dominating roles they are assigned.

When men step out of these dominating roles, there is often a violent response. Visible gay men are the objects of extreme hatred and fear by heterosexual men because they break ranks with male heterosexual solidarity and threaten the very fabric of male domination. The system can maintain itself only if gender relations are rigidly structured and controlled. This is done through strict gender roles, through the institutions of traditional marriage and the nuclear family, and through mandated heterosexuality.

The fifth theological challenge that gay and lesbian lives pose to the church has to do with gender and incarnational reality. Many of us believe that heterosexism is a form of idolatry. It is a system of domination that renders gay and lesbian lives utterly invisible, economically and socially oppressed, relationally disenfranchised. It is a system of human relatedness that presumes to represent all of human experience and reality.

Patricia Jung and Ralph Smith say it well: "By reducing sexuality to male-female dichotomies, heterosexism creates an idolatrous focus on one part of the whole. Idolatry occurs when anyone or anything is invested with more significance than is fitting. As an interpretive framework, heterosexism is itself idolatry."[20] Our narrow gender constructions are idolatrous. They do not adequately reflect the diversity of ways human beings express their humanity, and they keep all of us from incarnating the fullness of who we can be.

Marilyn Frye, a feminist lesbian theorist who writes a great deal about sex marking, sex identifying, and sex announcing as mandatory behaviors all of us are expected to engage in throughout our lives, reveals in a humorous, yet poignant way the idolatrous nature of rigidly maintained gender constructions:

> It is quite a spectacle, really, once one sees it, these humans so devoted to dressing up and acting out and "fixing" one another so everyone lives up to and lives out the theory that there are two sharply distinct sexes and never the twain shall overlap or be confused or conflated; these hominids constantly and with remarkable lack of embarrassment marking a distinction between two sexes as though their lives depended on it. It is wonderful that homosexuals and lesbians are mocked and judged for "playing butch-femme roles" and for dressing in "butch-femme drag," for nobody goes about in full public view as thoroughly decked out in butch and femme drag as respectable heterosexuals when they are dressed up to go out in the evening, or go to church, or go to the office. Heterosexual critics of queers' "roleplaying" ought to look at themselves in the mirror on their way out for a night on the town to see who's in drag. The answer is, everybody is. Perhaps the main difference between heterosexuals and queers is that when queers go forth in drag,

they know they are engaged in theater—they are playing and they know they are playing. Heterosexuals usually are taking it all perfectly seriously, thinking they are in the real world, thinking they *are* the real world.[21]

Frye's words confront religious people with frightening truth. Many gay and lesbian people believe in very profound ways that gender roles, the societal construction of manhood and womanhood, and blatant and constant gender announcing are the results of a system of power and control that are less than God's full intentions for humanity. Drag, theater, constructions of our own making, are just that, constructions of our own human making, not necessarily God's incarnational intentions. Many of us have so fundamentally accepted gender identity, gender roles, and gender distinctions as reality that these dimensions of our human experience have become some of the most poignant faces of idolatry. This expression of idolatry has many faces. Some of them are repressive and violent.

In *Gender Shock*, Phyllis Burke exposes the psychiatric practice in this country of diagnosing and treating gender identity disorder, in which children as young as three years old undergo "therapy," both at home and at school, for not adhering to accepted notions of "girl" and "boy" behavior.[22] Government records alone indicate that since the early 1970s, at least $1.5 million has been awarded from the National Institute of Mental Health to various organizations sponsoring studies and experiments on children who do not fit gender norms.[23] In the treatment, punitive responses, hospitalization, behavioral modification therapy, and psychiatric drugs have been used to modify the children's inappropriate gender behavior. There is even the Feminine Boy Project run by the University of California, Los Angeles.[24] Instead of gender being seen as something socially constructed, with socially sanctioned justifications, gender roles and identity have come to be understood by many as the essential nature of reality.

These rigid and idolatrous constructs of gender are enculturated into every male and female person in our society, even if violent, repressive means are deemed necessary. These gender constructs do not serve the health and well-being of women and men; they serve the oppressive institutions of sexism and heterosexism. Burke says: "It is my belief that by looking at what society pathologizes, we can see the clearest common denominator of what society demands of those of us who wish to be considered normal."[25] Gender nonconformity must be pathologized because gay and lesbian lives and homoerotic love must be pathologized. It is no accident that ultimately, gender identity disorder in almost every case comes to be closely associated with the child's sexuality and growing sexual orientation. Growing gay and lesbian children do not just live in the midst of smothering blankets of silence; they live as those who are medicated, actively punished, turned over to medical personnel by parents, and abandoned in hospitals. These are some of the human faces of gender idolatry or incarnational idolatry.

Many lesbian and gay people believe that no absolutes about gender are divinely ordained, that nothing about gender distinction must inherently dictate our fundamental humanness. Many of us believe that an unquestioning acceptance of rigid gender constructions fundamentally places us in direct opposition to the ultimate incarnational possibility and power of God. God's incarnational presence and power will not be restricted by our gender definitions. Gay and lesbian people do not just symbolize and embody sexual lives that depart from heterosexuality; we embody a different anthropology, a different humanness, that does not and will not accept all the many ways gender has been defined and constructed as normative for human life.

A Promised Place: Sleeping in the Woods Unafraid

Many lesbian and gay religious people are committed to building a world where gender ceases to be what silences, shames, restricts, and imprisons, and what maintains male dominance and heterosexual privilege. We are striving for a world where gender becomes the incarnational category for all that we can be, all that we can feel, all that we can experience, all that we can embody. If we are really serious about lesbian and gay voices transforming the church, if we are serious about preaching justice as lesbian and gay people, and in solidarity with that same community, we will be challenged to deconstruct what appears to be the most fundamental of all human categories, gender.

In that deconstructive process, we may just find God's incarnation power in ways we have never been able to imagine. In this world, where gender ceases to rule and heterosexism ceases to control, God's promise, through Ezekiel's words as they appear in chapter 34, might well become a promise for us all. All could sleep in the woods unafraid; all would have, and be, God's blessing; no one would be plundered and violated by another; the yoke of each and every one would be broken; and holy safety would be known by all. May God give us the courage to embrace this eschatological vision as it comes to us through the shockingly bold and sometimes heroic witness of lesbian and gay lives.

Images of Resistance and Hope

I T IS AN ENORMOUS challenge for one author to write an appropriate conclusion to a volume that includes eight diverse authors and preachers. The very purpose of this volume is to highlight the distinctive and individual voices of these authors-preachers, and to allow these voices to touch our lives directly. Any final summary on my part as the editor would be a violation of the book's contribution and intention.

Rather than summarize or interpret, I want to end this volume by lifting up the images and metaphors for preaching justice that are so artfully named and constructed by the authors. It seems fitting that the reader be left with these individual and collective images, and that any and all preachers who read this volume might feel their faithful indictment and their hope.

In chapter 1, Kathy Black, writing from the perspective of a person with a disability and rooted within the larger community of persons with disabilities, asserts:

> We can preach justice by carefully considering how we interpret the biblical texts that deal with someone being cured from a disability. . . .
> We can proclaim a God who does not cause disabilities but is able to transform our lives in the midst of them. We can help people encounter the face of God in someone maneuvering a wheelchair with an elbow or giving a lecture in sign language.

And she leaves us with a visionary image for the future and a clear picture of the world created by preaching justice:

> Justice will come when preaching is imaged as signing hands and animated bodies and when the perceived "broken bodies" of individuals are accepted in the holy sanctuary where the body of Christ is broken.

May all of our preaching help bring about such a day.

In chapter 2, Martin Brokenleg, writing from the perspective of one who is a Native person and rooted within the larger Lakota Nation, makes a claim:

> Essentially, then, the major images used to preach justice in Native communities include the healing ministry of Jesus, the cultural traditions as Old Testament, and the love of God for those considered the least in the world.

And he leaves us with a clear articulation of what preachers of justice must do in contexts of Native communities:

> A preacher of justice for Native people will proclaim triumph over the dynamics of racism, cultural discrimination, broken treaties, and social injustices toward ethnic minorities. . . . A loving preacher will connect Native people with our cultural traditions and through this unite us to the loving God.

May all of our preaching be in solidarity with such acts of denunciation and love.

In chapter 3, Teresa Fry Brown, writing from the perspective of one who is an African American woman and rooted within the larger African American community, draws upon Zora Neale Hurston to put before us a truth and a mandate:

> The Black church may be "sorrow's kitchen," or it may be the "peaky mountain" with the rainbows, harp, and sword. . . . "Sorrow's kitchen" must be renovated within any church and within any society that would oppress any segment of the community.

And she leaves us with a picture of what the church might look like when "sorrow's kitchen" is thoroughly renovated, and justice is preached:

> The "peaky mountain" is the place where God who is "no respecter of persons" resides and where African American women may "sit at the welcome table" with African American men. . . . This "peaky mountain" is the location of Black women singing God's praises unafraid and unashamed of the results. In faithfulness to a call from God these women—ordained and nonordained—"break the bread of life" for the freedom and salvation of the whole body.

May all of our preaching help renovate the places of sorrow and injustice within which people still reside.

In chapter 4, Eleazar S. Fernandez, writing from the perspective of one who is Filipino and rooted within the larger community of Filipino people, states:

> This "melting furnace" is not the melting pot of assimilation, but a furnace that burns our idols of death, purges us of our bigotry, and energizes us to continue struggling for a reconciled relationship. Out of this context and spirit Asian American preachers speak of the "fire of hope."

And he leaves us with this vivid depiction of the passionate work of justice-seeking Asian American preachers:

> Though they have settled in this land, they still embody the exilic journey of being both insiders and outsiders; of continuously search-ing for their identity in a pluralistic society; of dreaming and hoping for a better tomorrow. . . . Asian American preachers have the im-mense task of articulating and giving voice to the *han* and hope of Asian Americans.

May all of our preaching point toward a better tomorrow and have a pro-found sense of an "unfinished" dream.

In chapter 5, Justo L. González, writing from the perspective of one who is a Cuban-born Hispanic American and rooted within the larger Hispanic community, reveals a painful, persistent truth:

> For a number of reasons, many of us are in lands far from those of our birth. No matter how eagerly we devote ourselves to building houses and planting gardens (Jer. 29:5), we must still sing "by the rivers of Babylon" (Ps. 137:1).

And he leaves us with a view of the liveliness of Hispanic preaching that promises to sustain and transform:

> It is lively because in it we encounter the living Word of God; because that Word engages our very lives in their deepest hopes and hurts; be-cause were it not for this preaching and the Word it conveys, our bones

would be dried up. It is lively because a sermon is not a text, but that almost unspeakable miracle in which the preacher, the congregation, and the Word of God engage one another in a never-ending conversation.

May all of our preaching be this lively, this relevant, and this salvific.

In chapter 6, Eunjoo Mary Kim, writing from the perspective of one who is Korean American and rooted within the larger Korean community, offers a critique:

> Most sermons that concentrate on the personal relationship with God are in danger of leading the listeners to ignore the sociopolitical roots of their problems without critical reflection. They often tranquilize the listeners' consciousness by giving them temporary relief rather than offering the liberating message of the gospel to challenge them to solve their problems.

And she leaves us with a vision of what transformed preaching might sound like and look like:

> At this juncture, Korean American preachers are called upon to sing a radically new song in this strange new land of the United States. Singing a new song is possible only when Korean American preaching is transformed into an eschatological event that creates a new vision for the future of the community from the perspective of God's saving story.

May all of our preaching engage people in the work of singing a new song and forging a new world.

In chapter 7, Stacy Offner, writing from the perspective of one who is Jewish and rooted within the larger Jewish community, puts forth a powerful reminder:

> Listen to those before whom you stand. Hear the experience, the pain, the injustice, the joys, the needs, the longings, of those before whom you stand. Only then is it time to give voice.

And she leaves us with the image of the preacher's voice as a voice of justice:

You will know you are ready to give voice when the voices of those who cannot speak are heard in your voice. You will know you are ready to give voice when you have prayed that you might preach. You will know you are ready to give voice when you have taken to heart the admonition to *Da Lifney Mi Atta Omed*, to "know before whom you stand." Only then will your voice be a preacher's voice. And the preacher's voice will be a voice of justice.

May all of our preaching be grounded in the sacred acts of listening and knowing.

In chapter 8, I write from the perspective of one who is a lesbian and rooted within the larger community of lesbian and gay people, lamenting:

For many lesbian and gay people the church has been our greatest source of fear. At times it has offered us community, life and hope, grace and resurrection, yet often at enormous costs. . . . Often lesbian and gay people experience the church as a primary agent of this repressive violence, promising life and hope on the one hand, yet ultimately silencing us on the other.

And I leave us with a God-given promise that just might be realized as we preach and live justice:

In this world, where gender ceases to rule and heterosexism ceases to control, God's promise, through Ezekiel's words as they appear in chapter 34, might become a promise for us all. All could sleep in the woods unafraid; all would have, and be, God's blessing; no one would be plundered and violated by another; the yoke of each and every one of us would be broken; and holy safety would be known by all.

May all of our preaching break yokes of oppression and create moments and places of holy safety.

Notes

1. A PERSPECTIVE OF THE DISABLED: TRANSFORMING IMAGES OF GOD, INTERDEPENDENCE, AND HEALING

1. See Harlan Lane, *When the Mind Hears: A History of the Deaf* (New York: Random House, 1984); Sherman Wilcox, ed., *American Deaf Culture* (Silver Spring, Md.: Linstok Press, 1989); and Carol Padden and Tom Humphries, *Deaf in America: Voices from a Culture* (Cambridge: Harvard University Press, 1988).

2. Some persons within the disability community take pride in being who they are, with whatever disability they have, and understand statements such as "I am a crip" to be both a personal acceptance of their physical reality and a political protest against those whose language covers up or tries to hide that part of their being in the world.

3. Ashley Montagu, *The Elephant Man: A Study in Human Dignity* (New York: Ballantine Books, 1973).

4. I have since learned that this style of preaching is not unique to the Deaf culture but can also be found in some Filipino, Hmong, Vietnamese, Haitian, and Native American preaching.

5. See Evans Crawford, *The Hum: Call and Response in African American Preaching* (Nashville: Abingdon Press, 1995).

6. See Fred Craddock, *As One Without Authority* (Nashville: Abingdon Press, 1979); Henry Grady Davis, *Design for Preaching* (Philadelphia: Fortress Press, 1958); Charles Rice, *Interpretation and Imagination* (Philadelphia: Fortress Press, 1970); and Richard Lischer, *A Theology of Preaching* (Nashville: Abingdon Press, 1981).

7. Jaroslav J. Pelikan and Helmut Lehmann, eds., *Luther's Works*, 55 vols. (St. Louis: Concordia Publishing House; Philadelphia: Fortress Press, 1955), 29:224.

8. Henry Steward Wilson, *The Speaking God: Luther's Theology of Preaching.* (Ann Arbor, Mich.: University Microfilms International, 1977), 1.

9. David Buttrick, *Homiletic: Moves and Structures* (Philadelphia: Fortress Press, 1987), 175.

10. Craddock, *As One Without Authority*, 34, 42.

11. Walter Brueggemann, *Finally Comes the Poet* (Minneapolis: Fortress Press, 1989), 49.

12. Harold Wilke is an ordained United Church of Christ minister who is the founder of the Healing Community and the author of *Creating a Caring Congregation* (Nashville: Abingdon Press, 1980).

13. Phrase from stanza 6, "O for a Thousand Tongues to Sing," Charles Wesley, in *United Methodist Hymnal* (Nashville: The United Methodist Publishing House, 1989), 57.

14. For a more detailed discussion of the difference between "healing" and "cure" see Kathy Black, *A Healing Homiletic: Preaching and Disabilities* (Nashville: Abingdon Press, 1996).

15. *The Interpreter's Bible: Matthew and Mark*, vol. 7 (Nashville: Abingdon Press, 1951), 820.

16. Eduard Schweizer, *The Good News According to Mark* (Atlanta: John Knox Press, 1977), 58.

17. *The Interpreter's Bible: Matthew and Mark*, 757.

2. A NATIVE AMERICAN PERSPECTIVE: "THAT THE PEOPLE MAY LIVE"

1. Edward Spicer, *A Short History of the Indians of the United States* (New York: D. Van Nostrand, 1969).

2. Robert F. Berkhofer Jr., *The White Man's Indian* (New York: Knopf, 1978).

3. Edward Lazarus, *Black Hills/White Justice* (New York: Harper Collins, 1991).

4. Virginia Driving Hawk Sneve, *That They May Have Life* (New York: Seabury, 1977).

5. Felix S. Cohen, *Handbook of Federal Indian Law* (Albuquerque: University of New Mexico Press, 1945).

6. Hazel W. Hertzberg, *The Search for an American Indian Identity* (Syracuse: Syracuse University Press, 1971).

7. Larry Brendtro, Martin Brokenleg, and Steve Van Bockern, *Reclaiming Youth at Risk* (Bloomington, Ind.: National Educational Services, 1990).

8. Peggy Beck, Anna Lee Walters, and Nia San Francisco, *The Sacred* (Tsaile, Ariz.: Navajo Community College Press, 1992).

9. Ella Deloria, *Speaking of Indians* (Vermillion: University of South Dakota Press, 1983).

10. Raymond J. DeMallie, ed., *The Sixth Grandfather* (Lincoln: University of Nebraska Press, 1984).

11. William Stolzman, S.J., *The Pipe and Christ* (Pine Ridge, S.Dak.: Red Cloud Indian School, 1986).

12. Steve Charleston, "The Old Testament of Native America," in *Lift Every Voice*, ed. Susan Thistlethwaite and Mary Potter Engel (San Francisco: HarperSanFrancisco, 1990).

13. Papers of the Inculturation Committee, Office of Native Concerns, Catholic Diocese of Rapid City, 1996.

14. Marla N. Powers, *Oglala Women* (Chicago: University of Chicago Press, 1986).

15. John E. Farley, *Majority-Minority Relations* (Edwardsville, Ill.: Southern Illinois University, 1988).

16. Doyle Arbogas, *Wounded Warriors* (Omaha: Little Turtle Publications, 1996).

3. AN AFRICAN AMERICAN WOMAN'S PERSPECTIVE: RENOVATING SORROW'S KITCHEN

1. Zora Neale Hurston, *Dust Tracks on a Road* (New York: Harper Perennial, 1991), 205.

2. Katie G. Cannon, "The Wounds of Jesus: Justification of Goodness in the Face of Manifold Evil," in *Katie's Canon: Womanism and the Soul of the Black Community* (New York: Continuum, 1995), 112.

3. Cheryl Townsend Gilkes, "Some Mother's Son and Some Father's Daughter: Gender and Biblical Language in Afro-Christian Worship Tradition," in *Shaping New Vision: Gender and Values in American Culture*, ed. Clarissa W. Atkinson, Constance H. Buchanan, and Margaret R. Miles (Ann Arbor: UMI Research Press, 1987), 75–95.

4. Ibid., 72–76.

5. Ibid. Katie Cannon, "Womanist Interpretation and Preaching in the Black Church," in *Katie's Canon*, 113–21. *Womanist* is an interpretation of the Black folk expression "you actin' womanish." The term has developed since 1985, primarily by a group of African American women academicians, to refer to the experiences of Black women in the struggle to overcome multidimensional oppression. Womanist scholars explore the everyday experiences of Black women and how those experiences are used to effect liberation for Black women, the Black family, Black church, and Black community. For this chapter, the section of the definition coined by Alice Walker is used: "Committed to the survival and wholeness of an entire people, community, male and female; traditionally universalist" (*In Search of Our Mothers' Gardens* [San Diego: Harcourt, Brace, and Jovanovich, 1983], ix).

6. Gilkes, "Some Mother's Son," 84–96.

7. Irene Jackson, "Black Women and Music: A Survey from Africa to the New World," in *The Black Woman Cross Culturally*, ed. Filomena Choma Steady (Cambridge: Shenkman, 1981), 398.

8. Jualynne Dodson, "Nineteenth-Century AME Preaching Women," in *Women in New Worlds*,

ed. Hildah F. Thomas and Rosemary Skinner Keller (Nashville: Abingdon, 1981), 276–78.

9. Jarena Lee, *Religious Experience and Journal of Mrs. Jarena Lee, Giving an Account of Her Call to Preach the Gospel*, ed. A. Lee Henderson (Nashville: AMEC Sunday School Union, Legacy Publishing, 1991).

10. Ibid.

11. Melva Costen, *African American Christian Worship* (Nashville: Abingdon Press, 1993), 91–109.

12. Ibid.

13. Hurston, *Dust Tracks*, 205.

14. Cannon, "Womanist Interpretation and Preaching," 326–37.

15. Ibid.

16. Judith Weisenfeld, "We Have Been Believers: Patterns of African American Women's Religiosity," in *This Far by Faith: Readings in African American Women's Religious Biography*, ed. Judith Weisenfeld and Richard Newman (New York: Routledge, 1996), 7.

17. Renita Weems, "Reading Her Way through the Struggle: African American Women and the Bible," in *Stony the Road We Trod: African American Biblical Interpretation*, ed. Cain Hope Felder (Minneapolis: Fortress Press, 1991), 57–77.

18. Ibid., 70.

19. Anna Julia Cooper, *A Voice from the South by a Black Woman from the South* (1892; reprint, New York: Negro Universities Press, 1969).

4. A Filipino Perspective: "Unfinished Dream" in the Land of Promise

1. Christine Smith, *Preaching as Weeping, Confession, and Resistance: Radical Responses to Radical Evil* (Louisville: Westminster/John Knox Press, 1992), 1–14; Arthur Van Seters, ed., *Preaching as a Social Act: Theology and Practice* (Nashville: Abingdon Press, 1988), 19; Fred B. Craddock, *Preaching* (Nashville: Abingdon Press, 1985), 47; Thomas Long and Edward Farley, eds., *Preaching as Theological Task: World, Gospel, Scripture* (Louisville: Westminster/John Knox Press, 1996).

2. Craddock, *Preaching*, 47.

3. Felix Wilfred, "The Language of Human Rights: An Ethical Esperanto?" in *Frontiers in Asian Christian Theology: Emerging Trends*, ed. R. S. Sugirtharajah (Maryknoll, N.Y.: Orbis, 1994), 210.

4. Craddock, *Preaching*, 47–49.

5. Peter Hodgson paraphrasing Heidegger from his essays "Building Dwelling Thinking" and ". . . Poetically Man Dwells . . . ," in *Poetry, Language, Thought*, trans. Albert Hofstadter (New York: Harper & Row, 1971). See Peter Hodgson, *God in History: Shapes of Freedom* (Nashville: Abingdon Press, 1989), 92.

6. *Women and Men in Asia, the Women Question in Asian Context* (Hong Kong: Asia Regional Office-World Student Federation, 1976), part 1, 102, cited in C. S. Song, *Theology from the Womb of Asia* (Maryknoll, N.Y.: Orbis, 1986), 116.

7. Van Seters, *Preaching as a Social Act*, 19.

8. C. S. Song, "Context and Revelation with One Stroke of an Asian Brush," in *Lift Every Voice: Constructing Christian Theologies from the Underside*, ed. Susan Brooks Thistlethwaite and Mary Potter Engels (San Francisco: Harper & Row, 1990), 66, 72.

9. Andrew Sung Park, *Racial Conflict and Healing: An Asian-American Theological Perspective* (Maryknoll, N.Y.: Orbis, 1996), 130.

10. Eleazar S. Fernandez, *Toward a Theology of Struggle* (Maryknoll, N.Y.: Orbis, 1994), 168.

11. R. B. J. Walker, *One World, Many Worlds: Struggles for a Just World Peace* (Boulder, Colo.: Lynne Rienner, 1988).

12. Ronald Takaki, *Strangers from a Different Shore: A History of Asian Americans* (New York: Penguin, 1989), 25; also Takaki, *A Different Mirror: A History of Multicultural America* (Boston: Little, Brown, 1993), 246–76.

13. Aurora Tompar-Tiu and Juliana Sustento-Seneriches, *Depression and Other Mental Health Issues: The Filipino American Experience* (San Francisco: Jossey-Bass, 1995).

14. Carlos Bulosan, cited in Takaki, *Strangers from a Different Shore*, 344.

15. Ibid., 316.

16. Deborah Woo, "The Gap between Striving and Achieving: The Case of Asian American Women," in *Race, Class, and Gender: An Anthology*, ed. Margaret Andersen and Patricia Hill Collins (Belmont, Calif.: Wadsworth, 1992), 192–96.

17. Park, *Racial Conflict and Healing*, 46.

18. Takaki, *Strangers from a Different Shore*, 316.

19. Nobuko Joanne Miyamoto, "What Are You?" *Amerasia* 1, no. 3 (1971), cited in Fumitaka Matsuoka, *Out of Silence: Emerging Themes in Asian American Churches* (Cleveland: United Church Press, 1995), 109–10.

20. Tompar-Tiu and Sustento-Seneriches, *Depression and Other Mental Health Issues*, 47.

21. Takaki, *A Different Mirror*, 427.

22. Carlos Bulosan, *America Is in the Heart: A Personal History* (1946; reprint, Seattle: University of Washington Press, 1973).

23. Jung Young Lee, *Korean Preaching: An Interpretation* (Nashville: Abingdon Press, 1997), 118.

24. Robert Allen Warrior, "A Native American Perspective: Canaanites, Cowboys, and Indians," in *Voices from the Margin: Interpreting the Bible in the Third World*, ed. R. S. Sugirtharajah (Maryknoll, N.Y.: Orbis, 1991). Native Americans, argues Allen Warrior, identify with the biblical Canaanites, not the conquering Israelites, in the exodus narrative.

25. Grace Sangkok Kim, "Asian North American Youth: A Ministry of Self-Identity and Pastoral Care," in *People on the Way: Asian North Americans Discovering Christ, Culture, and Community*, ed. David Ng (Valley Forge, Pa.: Judson Press, 1996), 203.

26. Elizabeth Tay, cited in Matsuoka, *Out of Silence*, 133.

27. Matsuoka, *Out of Silence*, 133.

28. Ibid., 134.

29. Ibid., 117–20.

30. Ibid., 124–25.

31. Janice Mirikitani, "Breaking Silence," in *Shedding Silence: Poetry and Prose* (Berkeley, Calif.: Celestial Arts, 1987), 35.

32. Quoted from a sermon by Dr. Lourdino Yuzon, "Love Fulfilling the Law," Cosmopolitan United Church of Christ, Dallas, Texas, October 6, 1996.

5. A HISPANIC PERSPECTIVE: BY THE RIVERS OF BABYLON

1. On preaching justice in Latino and Latin American Protestant churches, see Daniel Rodríguez and Rodolfo Espinosa, eds., *Púlpito cristiano y justicia social* (Coyoacán, México: El Faro, 1994).

2. There is a conscious attempt to develop not so much a "method" as some "pointers," in Justo L. González and Catherine G. González, *The Liberating Pulpit* (a revised and expanded edition of *Liberation Preaching*) (Nashville: Abingdon Press, 1994), 66–95. Yet it was Pablo A. Jiménez who made me aware of the manner in which I have been actually correlating relationships in my biblical hermeneutics, in a way similar to what Clodovis Boff calls a "correspondence of relationships." Pablo A. Jiménez, "The Use of the Bible in Hispanic Theology" (D.Min. thesis, Columbia Theological Seminary, 1995), 84–89. Jiménez now teaches homiletics at the Episcopal Theological Seminary of the Southwest in Austin, Texas.

3. A point made earlier in Justo L. González and Catherine G. González, *Liberation Preaching: The Pulpit and the Oppressed* (Nashville: Abingdon Press, 1980), 97–98.

4. *Santa Biblia: The Bible through Hispanic Eyes* (Nashville: Abingdon Press, 1996).

5. The classical study in the field of religion and theology is Virgilio Elizondo's *Galilean Journey: The Mexican-American Promise* (Maryknoll, N.Y.: Orbis, 1983).

6. See, for instance, Orlando Costas, "Evangelism from the Periphery: A Galilean Model," *Apuntes* 2 (1982): 51–59, and "Evangelism from the Periphery: The Universality of Galilee," *Apuntes* 2 (1982): 75–84. Also Francisco García-Treto, "The Lesson of the Gibeonites: A Proposal for Dia-

logic Attention as a Strategy for Reading the Bible," in *Hispanic/Latino Theology: Challenge and Promise*, ed. Ada María Isasi-Díaz and Fernando Segovia (Minneapolis: Fortress Press, 1996), 73–85.

6. A Korean American Perspective: Singing a New Song in a Strange Land

1. Rev. Yong-Gee Cho is the senior pastor of Yoido Full Gospel Church in Seoul, which is the largest Protestant church in the world.

2. Steve S. Shim, *Korean Immigrant Churches Today in Southern California* (San Francisco: R and E Research Associates, 1977), 5–8.

3. Jung Ha Kim, *Bridge-Makers and Cross-Bearers: Korean-American Women and the Church* (Atlanta: Scholars Press, 1997), 7.

4. Ibid.

5. Won Moo Hurh and Kwang Chung Kim, *Korean Immigrants in America: A Structural Analysis of Ethnic Confinement and Adhesive Adaptation* (Rutherford, N.J.: Farleigh Dickinson University Press, 1984), 130.

6. Jung Ha Kim, *Bridge-Makers*, 14.

7. Paul Lehmann, *Ethics in a Christian Context* (New York: Harper & Row, 1963), 85.

8. Paul Lehmann, "The Christian Doctrine of Man III: Man as Believer," *Journal of Religious Thought* 2, no. 2 (1945): 179–94.

9. Eunjoo Mary Kim, "The Preaching of Transfiguration: Theology and Method of Eschatological Preaching as an Alternative to Contemporary Korean Preaching" (Ph.D. diss., Princeton Theological Seminary, 1996), 161–62.

10. Ibid., 145; Nancy J. Duff, *Humanization and the Politics of God: The Koinonia Ethics of Paul Lehmann* (Grand Rapids, Mich.: Eerdmans, 1992), 10.

11. Eunjoo Mary Kim, "The Preaching of Transfiguration," 144.

12. I collected as many Korean American preachers' sermon books as I could from Korean American Christian bookstores in Los Angeles, New York City, Washington, D.C., Chicago, and Fort Lee, New Jersey. The books I collected and reviewed are as follows: Jong-Chan Chang, *Expand the Lot* (Seoul: Cummran Publishing Co., 1995); Hyo-Sup Choi, *The Joy of Love* (Seoul: Voice Publishing Co., 1995); the Council of the Korean-American Church in New Jersey, *Those Who Crossed the Sea* (Seoul: Voice Publishing Co., 1995); the Council of the Korean Presbyterian Church in West, *The Heavenly Door Is Opening* (Seoul: Word of Life Publishing Co., 1994); Min-Oong Kim, *The Bread Sent Out Upon Waters* (Seoul: Institute of Korean Theology, 1995); Dong-Won Lee, *For the Sake of Joyful Life* (Seoul: Nachimban Ministries Co., 1996); Sungnak Paul Lee, *Grace Which You See with Eyes* (Seoul: Kulmarum Co., 1996); Yong-Jae Lee, *The Well Dug in the Wilderness* (Seoul: Star Publishing Co., 1993); Dong-Sun Yim, *You Reap Whatever You Sow* (Seoul: Word of Life Publishing Co., 1996); Samuel Yun, *Living the Prayer* (Seoul: Voice Publishing Co., 1994). Among them, the most helpful in understanding the general trends of contemporary Korean American preaching were *Those Who Crossed the Sea*, a collection of forty pastors' sermons from various denominations preached in New Jersey churches, and *The Heavenly Door Is Opening*, a collection of sermons written by twenty pastors of the Korean Presbyterian Church in California.

13. Tae-Ho Ahn, "The Lord Is Waiting for You," in *Those Who Crossed the Sea*, 212. (The translation is mine.)

14. Jung Young Lee, *Korean Preaching: An Interpretation* (Nashville: Abingdon Press, 1997), 80.

15. Sang-Kyu Kim, "The Secret of Blessing," in *The Heavenly Door Is Opening*, 54–55. (The translation is mine.)

16. Ann-Janine Morey-Gaines, *Apples and Ashes* (Chico, Calif.: Scholars Press, 1982), 2.

17. Hyo-Sup Choi, "The Procession to Jerusalem," in *The Joy of Love*, 114. (The translation is mine.)

18. E.g., Sung-Ji Kim, "The Standard Church," in *The Heavenly Door Is Opening*, 122–34.

19. Dong-Sun Yim, "The Construction of the Temple," in *You Reap Whatever You Sow*, 163–72.

20. United States Commission on Civil Rights, *Civil Rights: Civil Rights Issues Facing Asian*

Americans in the 1990s (Washington, D.C.: U.S. Commission on Civil Rights,1992), 182.

21. Jung Ha Kim, *Bridge-Makers*, 98.

22. Andrew Sung Park, *Racial Conflict and Healing: An Asian-American Theological Perspective* (Maryknoll, N.Y.: Orbis, 1996), 28.

23. Elaine H. Kim, "Between Black and White: An Interview with Bong Hwan Kim," in *The State of Asian America: Activism and Resistance in the 1990s*, ed. Karin Aguilar-San Juan (Boston: South End Press, 1994), 90.

24. United States Commission on Civil Rights, *Civil Rights*, 19.

25. Ibid., 23–24.

26. Ibid., 19.

27. Quoted from Andrew Sung Park, *Racial Conflict and Healing*, 38, and Cornel West, *Race Matters* (New York: Vintage Books, 1994), 10–11.

28. Doug Henwood, "American Dream: It's Not Working," *Christianity and Crisis* 52 (1992): 195.

29. William Tabb, "The Crisis of the Present Economic System and Renewing the American Dream," in *Theology in the Americas: Detroit II Conference Papers*, ed. Probe (Maryknoll, N.Y.: Orbis, 1982), 31.

30. United States Commission on Civil Rights, *Civil Rights*, 173.

31. Ibid., 72.

32. Won Moo Hurh and Kwang Chung Kim, *Korean Immigrants in America*, 140.

33. Jung Young Lee, *Korean Preaching*, 122.

34. Fred Craddock, *Preaching* (Nashville: Abingdon Press, 1987), 90.

35. Eunjoo Mary Kim, "The Preaching of Transfiguration," 179, 186.

36. Jung Young Lee, *Marginality: The Key to the Multicultural Theology* (Minneapolis: Fortress Press, 1995), 52.

37. Ibid., 60.

38. Ibid., 63.

39. Paul Lehmann, *The Decalogue and a Human Future: The Meaning of the Commandments for Making and Keeping Human Life Human* (Grand Rapids, Mich.: Eerdmans, 1995), 85.

40. Eunjoo Mary Kim, "The Preaching of Transfiguration," 245–47.

7. A JEWISH PERSPECTIVE: PURSUING JUSTICE THROUGH KNOWLEDGE OF SELF AND OTHERS

1. Chaim Stern, ed., *Gates of Prayer: The New Union Prayerbook* (New York: Central Conference of American Rabbis, 1975), 3.

2. Rabbi Jacob Philip Rudin, *Very Truly Yours: A Harvest of Forty Years in the Pulpit* (New York: Bloch Publishing Co., 1971), vii.

3. See *Webster's New World Dictionary* (New York: World Publishing Co., 1966).

4. Cynthia Ozick, "Note Toward Finding the Right Question," in *On Being a Jewish Feminist*, ed. Susannah Heschel (New York: Schocken, 1983), 125; reprinted from *Lilith* magazine, no. 6, 1979.

5. I am indebted to Judith Plaskow for this insight, which she shared with a gathering of female rabbis at the Women's Rabbinic Network conference in Washington, D.C., in the spring of 1984.

6. Excerpted from the Mission Statement of Shir Tikvah Congregation, 1988.

7. Sermon preached at Shir Tikvah Congregation, December 18, 1992.

8. Sermon preached at Shir Tikvah Congregation, March 2, 1996.

9. I use the phrase "sermon manuscript" quite intentionally here, for the written words on the page are not the whole of the sermon. The sermon itself is a moment in time and comprises all the aforementioned factors and more (e.g., words, preacher, relationship, baggage, etc.).

10. *Halacha* is a Hebrew word meaning "the path." It is a word in Judaism that indicates the realm of Jewish law.

11. All biblical quotations cited in this chapter come from *TANAKH—The Holy Scriptures: The New JPS Translation according to the Traditional Hebrew Text* (Philadelphia: Jewish Publication Society, 1988), unless otherwise noted.

12. Leonard Fein, *Where Are We?* (New York: Harper & Row, 1988), 26.

13. Menachoth 43b.

14. See, for example, Carol Christ and Judith Plaskow, eds., *Womanspirit Rising: A Feminist Reader in Religion* (San Francisco: Harper & Row, 1979); Rachel Biale, *Women and Jewish Law: An Exploration of Women's Issues in Halakhic Sources* (New York: Schocken, 1984); Susannah Heschel, ed., *On Being a Jewish Feminist.*

15. Biale, *Women and Jewish Law*, 9.

16. B. S. Jacobson, *The Weekday Siddur: An Exposition and Analysis of Its Structure, Contents, Language and Ideas* (Tel Aviv: Sinai Publishing, 1978), 42.

17. Moshe Meiselman, *Jewish Woman in Jewish Law* (New York: Ktav, 1978), 43–44.

18. Harold Kushner, *To Life!* (Boston: Little, Brown, 1993), 261.

19. Martin Niemoeller, a pastor in the German Confessing Church who spent eight and a half years in a concentration camp. Printed in Elie Wiesel and Albert Friedlander, *The Six Days of Destruction* (Mahwah, N.J.: Paulist Press, 1988), 93.

20. Emil Fackenheim, "The 614th Commandment," in *Holocaust*, ed. John Roth and Michael Berenbaum (New York: Paragon House, 1989), 294.

21. Gunther Plaut, *The Torah: A Modern Commentary* (New York: Union of American Hebrew Congregations, 1981), 1461.

22. Bachya Ben Asher, quoted in Urbach, *The Sages*, quoted in Plaut, *The Torah*, 1462.

23. Everett Fox, *The Five Books of Moses* (New York: Schocken, 1995), 927.

24. Jerome Chanes, "Public Policy and Tikkun Olam," *The Reconstructionist* 61, no. 1 (spring 1966): 59.

8. A LESBIAN PERSPECTIVE: MOVING TOWARD A PROMISED PLACE

1. These thoughts are more fully developed in my book *Preaching as Weeping, Confession, and Resistance: Radical Responses to Radical Evil* (Louisville: Westminster/John Knox Press, 1992) and in the article "Preaching as an Art of Resistance," in *The Arts of Ministry: Feminist/Womanist Approaches*, ed. Christie Neuger (Louisville: Westminster/John Knox Press, 1996).

2. Mitsuye Yamada, *Desert Run: Poems and Stories* (Latham, N.Y.: Kitchen Table—Women of Color Press, 1988), 55.

3. Carter Heyward, *Touching Our Strength: The Erotic as Power and the Love of God* (San Francisco: Harper & Row, 1989), 47.

4. Gary Remafedi, ed., *Death by Denial: Studies of Suicide in Gay and Lesbian Teenagers* (Boston: Alyson Publications, 1994). This book documents several studies, including a 1989 federal study, that discovered that teenagers who were struggling with issues of sexual orientation were three times more likely to commit suicide than their peers.

5. John E. Fortunato, *Embracing the Exile: Healing Journeys of Gay Christians* (San Francisco: Harper & Row, 1982). See this volume for a thorough discussion of the metaphor of exile as it relates to lesbian and gay lives.

6. Carter Heyward, *Speaking of Christ: A Lesbian Feminist Voice*, ed. Ellen C. Davis (New York: Pilgrim Press, 1989), 20.

7. See Phyllis Trible's work *Texts of Terror: Literary-Feminist Readings of Biblical Narratives* (Philadelphia: Fortress Press, 1984). Even though her emphasis in this book is on texts of terror that depict violence against women and how to bring a critical hermeneutic to those texts, many of the insights are applicable to a hermeneutic seeking to address the texts that continue to rigidly reinforce heterosexism, and the texts that justify homophobic hate.

8. See Gary David Comstock, *Gay Theology Without Apology* (Cleveland: Pilgrim Press, 1993), and Nancy Wilson, *Our Tribe: Queer Folks, God, Jesus, and the Bible* (San Francisco: HarperCollins, 1985).

9. An important volume for making many of these connections is *A Certain Terror: Heterosexism, Militarism, Violence, and Change*, ed. Richard Cleaver and Patricia Myers (Chicago: Great Lakes Region American Friends Service Committee, 1993).

10. Chris Glaser, *Come Home! Reclaiming Spirituality and Community as Gay Men and Les-*

bians (San Francisco: Harper & Row, 1990), 180.

11. This insight was shared by Myles Alexander within a sermon at Spirit of the Lakes United Church of Christ, Minneapolis.

12. Comstock, *Gay Theology Without Apology*, 16–17.

13. Essex Hemphill, *Brother to Brother: New Writings by Gay Men* (Boston: Alyson Productions, 1991), xvi.

14. bell hooks, *Yearning: Race, Gender, and Cultural Politics* (Boston: South End Press, 1990), 148–49.

15. Ibid., 149.

16. Jack Pantaleo, "The Opened Tomb," *The Other Side*, March–April 1992, 11–12.

17. Robert Goss, *Jesus Acted Up: A Gay and Lesbian Manifesto* (San Francisco: Harper, 1993), xvii.

18. Pantaleo, "The Opened Tomb," 8.

19. Julia Penelope and Susan J. Wolfe, eds., *The Coming Out Stories* (Freedom, Calif.: Crossing Press, 1980), 4.

20. Patricia Beattie Jung and Ralph F. Smith, *Heterosexism: An Ethical Challenge* (Albany: State University of New York Press, 1993), 107.

21. Marilyn Frye, *The Politics of Reality: Essays in Feminist Theory* (Freedom, Calif.: Crossing Press, 1983), 29.

22. Phyllis Burke, *Gender Shock: Exploding the Myths of Male and Female* (New York: Anchor, 1996).

23. Ibid., 32–33.

24. Ibid., 32.

25. Ibid., 4.